Appetizers, Starters & Finger Food

Appetizers, Starters & Finger Food

200 great ways to start a meal or serve a buffet with style:
step-by-step recipes for guaranteed success

consultant editor
christine ingram

JG PRESS

Published by World Publications Group, Inc.
140 Laurel Street
East Bridgewater, MA 02333
www.wrldpub.net

Produced by Anness Publishing Ltd
Hermes House, 88–89 Blackfriars Road, London SE1 8HA
tel. 020 7401 2077; fax 020 7633 9499
www.annesspublishing.com

If you like the images in this book and would like to investigate using them for publishing, promotions or advertising, please visit our website
www.practicalpictures.com for more information.

Publisher: Joanna Lorenz
Editor: Charlotte Berman
Designer: Bill Mason
Jacket Design: Balley Design
Illustrator: Anna Koska
Editorial Reader: Diane Ashmore
Production Controller: Wendy Lawson
Recipes: Catherine Atkinson, Alex Barker, Steve Baxter, Angela Boggiano, Carla Capalbo, Kit Chan, Jacqueline Clarke, Maxine Clarke, Andi Cleveley, Roz Denny,
Joanne Farrow, Rafi Fernandez, Silvano Franco, Christine France, Sarah Gates, Shirley Gill, Nicola Graimes, Rosamund Grant, Carole Handslip, Deh-Ta Hsiung,
Peter Jordan, Elisabeth Lambert Ortiz, Ruby Le Bois, Clare Lewis, Sara Lewis, Leslie Mackley, Norma MacMillan, Sally Mansfield, Sue Maggs, Sallie Morris,
Jenny Stacey, Liz Trigg, Hilaire Walden, Laura Washburn, Steven Wheeler, Kate Whiteman, Elizabeth Wolf-Cohen, Jeni Wright
Photography: Karl Adamson, Edward Allwright, Steve Baxter, James Duncan, John Freeman, Ian Garlick, Michelle Garrett, Peter Henley, John Heseltine,
Janine Hosegood, Amanda Heywood, David Jordan, Maria Kelly, Dave King, Don Last, William Lingwood, Patrick McLeavey, Michael Michaels, Thomas Odulate, Sam Stowell

ETHICAL TRADING POLICY
At Anness Publishing we believe that business should be conducted in an ethical and ecologically sustainable way, with respect for the environment and
a proper regard to the replacement of the natural resources we employ.
As a publisher, we use a lot of wood pulp to make high-quality paper for printing, and that wood commonly comes from spruce trees. We are therefore currently
growing more than 750,000 trees in three Scottish forest plantations: Berrymoss (130 hectares/320 acres), West Touxhill (125 hectares/305 acres) and Deveron Forest
(75 hectares/185 acres). The forests we manage contain more than 3.5 times the number of trees employed each year in making paper for the books we manufacture.
Because of this ongoing ecological investment program, you, as our customer, can have the pleasure and reassurance of knowing that a tree is being cultivated
on your behalf to naturally replace the materials used to make the book you are holding.
Our forestry programme is run in accordance with the UK Woodland Assurance Scheme (UKWAS) and will be certified by the internationally recognized
Forest Stewardship Council (FSC). The FSC is a non-government organization dedicated to promoting responsible management of the world's forests.
Certification ensures forests are managed in an environmentally sustainable and socially responsible way.
For further information about this scheme, go to www.annesspublishing.com/trees

ISBN-10: 1-57215-502-7
ISBN-13: 978-1-57215-502-2

Printed and bound in China

Previously published as *Appetizers, Starters & Hors d'Oeuvres*

NOTES

Standard spoon and cup measures are level.

Large eggs are used unless otherwise stated.

Electric oven temperatures in this book are for conventional ovens. When using a fan oven, the temperature will probably need to be reduced by about 20–40°F.
Since ovens vary, you should check with your manufacturer's instruction book for guidance.

CONTENTS

Introduction

For many people appetizers are the best part of a meal. Indeed, they are so popular, that sometimes whole dinner parties consist entirely of a variety of appetizers. You can see the attraction—appetizers by definition mean small portions, which means there can be a huge and delicious selection of different dishes. Of course for the cook, providing such a medley of diverse foods can be quite a challenge, (although one you may well feel equal to), but for the guests it will be nothing less than a complete delight!

In some countries, appetizers have become an institution. Tapas, in Spain, are a meal in their own right, and Italian antipasto is so varied and delicious that you'd be forgiven for wishing to stop right there with the artichokes and superb dried hams, and forget entirely about the pasta and meat that follow.

The list of different appetizers is almost endless. If you're planning a sophisticated dinner party, it is possible to start with a simple but tasty appetizer such as Marinated Olives or Pork and Peanut Wontons with Plum Sauce, which can be served easily beforehand with drinks. Your choice of appetizer should take its cue from the food you intend to serve as a main course. You need to choose this with care, as the appetizer will set the tone for the rest of the meal. Select something fairly light, such as Grilled Jumbo Shrimp or a simple salad if you plan to serve a roast meat or hearty stew. If, on the other hand, you are grilling fish or chicken, you could decide on something more elaborate. Vegetable or fish terrines look pretty and taste wonderful, or choose from one of the many special occasion appetizers. For an Asian meal, you could make a Thai-style soup, or serve Chicken Satay with Peanut Sauce. However, don't feel too constrained by the ethnicity of your meal. Today, the trend is to serve foods that complement each other. A Mediterranean-style appetizer such as Charred Artichokes with Lemon Oil Dip could happily come before an Indonesian green curry. Similarly, Malayan Shrimp Laksa would be fine before a French or Italian-style meal. Those rules that do exist are concerned with texture and taste. For example, if you're making a soufflé or roulade as a main course, choose something crisp as an appetizer.

There is something for every occasion in this book, and whether it's soups or nibbles, party food or family favorites, you are bound to be inspired to start a meal in the best possible way.

Garnishes

Many garnishes are delicate works of art that seem almost a shame to eat, and others add a dash of texture or a hint of color without which the dish would just not be the same.

CREAM SWIRL

Pour in a swirl of cream, sour cream or yogurt to make a bowl of soup look particularly attractive.

To create a delicate pattern, draw the tip of a fine skewer back and forth through the swirl.

CROÛTONS

Croutons are an easy and effective way to use up stale bread while adding crunch to any dish, and are always served with gazpacho and Caesar salad.

1 Once you have cut your chosen bread into small cubes, either fry them in sunflower oil until they are golden and crisp, or brush them with oil and bake. They will keep in an airtight container for up to a week.

CUCUMBER FLOWERS

This is a stunning garnish that would grace any dinner party.

1 Cut the cucumber in half lengthwise and remove the seeds. Place each half cut-side down and then cut at an angle into 3-inch lengths. Cut into fine slices stopping ¼ inch short of the far side, so that the slices remain attached.

2 Fan the slices out. Turn in alternate slices to form a loop. Bend the length into a semicircle so the cucumber loops resemble the petals of a flower.

LEMON TWIST

A classic garnish—so simple but very effective.

Cut a lemon into ¼-inch slices. Make a cut in each slice from the center to the skin. Hold the slice on either side of the cut and twist to form an "S" shape.

PARMESAN CURLS

Curls of Parmesan add a delicate touch to pasta or risotto.

Holding a swivel-bladed peeler at a 45° angle, draw it steadily across the block of Parmesan cheese to form a curl.

CHILE FLOWERS

Make these chile flowers several hours before needed to let the "flowers" open up.

1 Use a small pair of scissors or a slim-bladed knife to cut a chile carefully lengthwise up from the tip to within ½ inch of the stem end. Repeat this at regular intervals around the chile—more cuts will produce more petals. Repeat with the remaining chiles.

2 Rinse the chiles in cold water and remove all the seeds. Place the chiles in a bowl of ice water and chill for at least 4 hours. For very curly flowers leave the chiles overnight.

CHIVE BRAIDS

Try floating a couple of edible braids of chives in a bowl of soup.

1 Align three chives on a work surface with a bowl on one end to hold them still. Carefully braid the chives together to within 1 inch of the end.

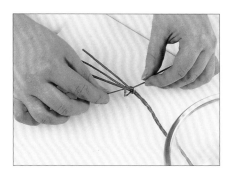

2 Tie a thin chive around the exposed end of the braid. Remove the bowl and tie the other end the same way. Trim both ends with kitchen scissors.

3 Plaice the braid in a bowl and pour boiling water onto it. Let stand for 20–30 seconds then drain and refresh under cold water. Drain again.

SCALLION TASSELS

You can often find this garnish at Chinese restaurants, where the appearance of a dish is almost as important as its taste.

Cut the white part of a scallion into a 2½-inch length. Shred one end of each piece, then place in ice water for about 30 minutes, until the ends curl.

TOMATO SUNS

Colorful cherry tomato suns look good with pâtés and terrines.

1 Place a tomato stem-side down. Cut lightly into the skin across the top, edging the knife down toward the bottom on either side. Repeat until the skin has been cut into eight separate segments, joined at the bottom.

2 Slide the top of the knife under the point of each segment and ease the skin away toward the bottom. Gently fold the petals back to mimic the sun's rays.

AVOCADO FAN

Avocados are amazingly versatile—they can serve as edible containers, be sliced or diced in a salad, or form the foundation of a delicious soup or sauce. They also make very elegant garnishes.

1 Halve, pit and peel an avocado. Slice each half lengthwise into quarters. Gently draw a zester across the quarters at ½-inch intervals, to create regular stripes.

2 Make four cuts lengthwise down each avocado quarter leaving ½ inch intact at the end. Carefully fan out the slices and arrange on a plate.

Marinades, Oils and Dressings

Marinades, flavored oils and dressings can turn a plain piece of fish or a sliced vegetable into a delectable appetizer, starter or hors d'oeuvre. With a few simple ingredients, and in just a few minutes, you can make a fresh herb marinade to tenderize fish or meat, a ginger and garlic oil for fragrant fried dishes and a sour cream dressing to bring out the flavor of crisp salad vegetables.

SUMMER HERB MARINADE

Make the best of summer herbs in this marinade. Any combination may be used depending on what you have on hand, and it works well with veal, chicken, pork or lamb.

1 Discard any coarse stalks or damaged leaves from a selection of herb sprigs, such as chervil, thyme, parsley, sage, chives, rosemary and oregano, then chop finely.

2 Mix the herbs with 6 tablespoons olive oil, 3 tablespoons tarragon vinegar, 1 garlic clove, crushed, 2 scallions, chopped, and salt and pepper. Add the meat or poultry, cover and chill for 2–3 hours.

GINGER AND LIME MARINADE

This refreshing marinade is particularly good with chicken.

1 Mix the zest of one lime and the juice of three limes. Add 1 tablespoon green cardamom seeds, crushed, 1 finely chopped onion, grated fresh ginger root (use a 1-inch piece and peel before grating), 1 large garlic clove, crushed and 3 tablespoons olive oil.

2 Pour onto the meat or fish. Stir gently to coat, cover and set in a cool place for 2–3 hours.

CHILE AND GARLIC MARINADE

Add extra chiles if you like your food to be very spicy.

1 Combine 4 small chiles, seeded and finely diced, 2 teaspoons finely grated fresh gingerroot, 1 large garlic clove, crushed, and 3 tablespoons light soy sauce in a bowl. Add the meat or fish, cover and chill for 2–4 hours.

CHINESE MARINADE

This marinade is traditionally used to flavor succulent duck breasts.

2 Mix 1 tablespoon honey, 1¼ teaspoons five spice powder, 1 garlic clove, finely chopped, 1 tablespoon hoisin sauce and a pinch of salt and pepper. Add the duck breasts or other meat, turning them in the marinade. Cover and set in a cool place to marinate for 2 hours.

AROMATIC SPICE OIL

As well as tasting delicious, aromatic oils make wonderful gifts. Ginger Garlic and Shallot Oil is simple and delicious, but you could also try using a combination of other spices and flavorings, such as chiles, coriander, lemongrass, peppercorns and lime leaves.

1 Peel and lightly bruise a 2½-inch piece of fresh gingerroot and place in a clean bottle. Fill with peanut oil, 2 garlic cloves (left whole) and 3 small peeled shallots. Cover tightly and set in a cool dark place for 2 weeks or until the flavor is sufficiently pronounced, before using.

PARSLEY, SAGE AND THYME OIL

Chop a handful each of fresh parsley, sage and thyme. Place in a bottle and fill up with olive oil. Seal and let stand at room temperature for about a week, shaking occasionally. Strain the oil into another sterilized, decorative bottle, discard the chopped herbs and add a fresh sprig or two to decorate.

SOUR CREAM AND DILL DRESSING

This unusual dressing can be made in only a couple of minutes.

1 Blend together ½ cup sour cream, 2 teaspoons creamed horseradish and 1 tablespoon chopped fresh dill in a small bowl and season with a little salt and pepper.

SPICY TOMATO DRESSING

This tangy dressing goes very well with a robust salad, such as bean or potato salad. It can also be used as a marinade.

1 Mix 1 teaspoon ground cumin, 1 tablespoon ketchup, 2 tablespoons olive oil, 1 tablespoon white wine vinegar and 1 garlic clove, crushed in a small bowl. Add a little salt and some hot pepper sauce to taste and stir again thoroughly.

HERB GARDEN DRESSING

The dried mixture will keep throughout the winter until your herbs are growing again. It can also be used to sprinkle on vegetables, casseroles and stews.

1 Mix 1 cup dried oregano, 1 cup dried basil, ½ cup dried marjoram, ½ cup dried dill weed, ½ cup dried mint leaves, ½ cup onion powder, 2 tablespoons dry mustard, 2 teaspoons salt and 1 tablespoon freshly ground black pepper and keep in a sealed jar to use as needed.

2 When making a batch of salad dressing, take 2 tablespoons of the herb mixture and add it to 1½ cups of extra virgin olive oil and ½ cup cider vinegar. Mix thoroughly and let stand for 1 hour or so. Mix again before using.

NIBBLES
AND DIPS

Marinated Olives

For the best flavor, marinate the olives for at least 10 days and serve at room temperature.

INGREDIENTS

Serves 4

1⅓ cups unpitted, green olives

3 garlic cloves

1 teaspoon coriander seeds

2 small red chiles

2–3 thick slices of lemon, cut into pieces

1 thyme or rosemary sprig

5 tablespoons white wine vinegar

1 Spread out the olives and garlic on a cutting board. Using a rolling pin, crack and flatten them slightly.

2 Crack the coriander seeds in a mortar with a pestle.

> ### COOK'S TIP
> ∼
> For a change, use a mix of caraway and cumin seeds instead of the coriander.

3 Mix the olives and the garlic, coriander seeds, chiles, lemon pieces, herb sprigs and white wine vinegar in a large bowl. Toss well, then transfer the mixture to a clean glass jar. Pour in cold water to cover. Store in the refrigerator for at least 5 days before serving at room temperature.

Salted Almonds

These crunchy salted nuts are at their best when fresh so, if you can, cook them on the day you plan to eat them.

INGREDIENTS

Serves 2–4

1 cup whole almonds in their skins

1 tablespoon egg white, lightly beaten

½ teaspoon coarse sea salt

> ### COOK'S TIP
> ∼
> This traditional method of salt-roasting nuts gives a matte, dry-looking finish; if you want them to shine, turn the roasted nuts into a bowl, add 1 tablespoon of olive oil and shake well to coat.

1 Preheat the oven to 350°F. Spread out the almonds on a baking sheet and roast for about 20 minutes, until cracked and golden.

2 Mix the egg white and salt in a bowl, add the almonds and shake well to coat.

3 Turn out onto the baking sheet, give a shake to separate the nuts, then return them to the oven for 5 minutes, until they have dried. Set aside until cold, then store in an airtight container until ready to serve.

Potato Skins with Cajun Dip

Divinely crisp, these potato skins are great on their own or served with this piquant dip as a garnish or on the side.

INGREDIENTS

Serves 4

2 large baking potatoes
vegetable oil, for deep-frying

For the dip

½ cup plain yogurt
1 garlic clove, crushed
1 teaspoon tomato paste or
   ½ teaspoon green chili purée or
   ½ small green chile, chopped
¼ teaspoon celery salt
salt and ground black pepper

1 Preheat the oven to 350°F. Bake the potatoes for 45–50 minutes, until tender. Cut them in half and scoop out the flesh, leaving a thin layer on the skins. Keep the flesh for another meal. Cut the potatoes in half once more.

2 To make the dip, combine all the ingredients and chill.

3 Heat a ½-inch layer of oil in a saucepan or deep-fat fryer. Fry the potatoes until crisp and golden on both sides. Drain on paper towels, then sprinkle with salt and black pepper. Serve the potato skins with a bowl of dip or a dollop of dip in each skin.

Celeriac Fritters with Mustard Dip

The combination of the hot, crispy fritters and cold mustard dip is extremely good.

INGREDIENTS

Serves 4

1 egg

1½ cups ground almonds

3 tablespoons freshly grated Parmesan cheese

3 tablespoons chopped fresh parsley

1 celeriac, about 1 pound

lemon juice

oil, for deep-frying

salt and ground black pepper

sea salt flakes, to garnish

For the dip

⅔ cup sour cream

1–2 tablespoons whole-grain mustard

1 Beat the egg well and pour into a shallow dish. Combine the almonds, grated Parmesan and parsley in a separate dish. Season with salt and plenty of ground black pepper. Set aside.

2 Peel and cut the celeriac into batons about ½-inch wide and 2-inches long. Drop them immediately into a bowl of water with a little lemon juice added to prevent discoloration.

3 Heat the oil to 350°F. Drain and then pat dry half the celeriac batons. Dip them into the beaten egg, then into the ground almond mixture, making sure that the pieces are coated completely and evenly.

4 Deep-fry the fritters, in batches, for 2–3 minutes until golden. Drain on paper towels. Keep warm while you cook the remaining fritters.

5 Make the dip. Mix the sour cream, mustard and salt to taste. Spoon into a serving bowl. Sprinkle the fritters with sea salt.

Chili Bean Dip

This deliciously spicy and creamy bean dip is best served warm with triangles of toasted pita bread or a bowl of crunchy tortilla chips.

INGREDIENTS

Serves 4

2 garlic cloves

1 onion

2 green chiles

2 tablespoons vegetable oil

1–2 teaspoons hot chili powder

14-ounce can kidney beans

3 ounces aged Cheddar cheese, grated

1 red chile, seeded

salt and ground black pepper

1 Finely chop the garlic and onion. Seed and finely chop the green chiles.

2 Heat the vegetable oil in a large sauté pan or deep frying pan and add the garlic, onion, green chiles and chili powder. Cook gently for about 5 minutes, stirring regularly, until the onions are softened and transparent, but not browned.

3 Drain the kidney beans, reserving the liquor. Blend all but 2 tablespoons of the beans into a purée in a food processor.

4 Add the puréed beans to the pan with 2–3 tablespoons of the reserved liquor. Heat gently, stirring to mix well.

5 Stir in the whole beans and the Cheddar cheese. Cook gently for 2–3 minutes, stirring until the cheese melts. Add salt and pepper to taste.

6 Cut the red chile into tiny strips. Spoon the dip into four individual serving bowls and sprinkle the chile strips on top. Serve warm.

COOK'S TIP

For a dip with a coarser texture, do not purée the beans; instead, mash them with a potato masher.

Lemon and Coconut Dhal Dip

A warm spicy dish, this can be served either as a dip with warmed pita bread or as an accompaniment to cold meats.

Serves 8

2-inch piece fresh ginger
1 onion
2 garlic cloves
2 small red chiles, seeded
2 tablespoons sunflower oil
1 teaspoon cumin seeds
²⁄₃ cup red lentils
1 cup water
1 tablespoon hot curry paste
scant 1 cup coconut cream
juice of 1 lemon
handful of cilantro leaves
¼ cup sliced almonds
salt and ground black pepper

1 Use a vegetable peeler to peel the ginger and finely chop it with the onion, garlic and chiles.

VARIATION

Try making this dhal with yellow split peas: they take longer to cook and a little extra water has to be added, but the results are equally tasty.

2 Heat the sunflower oil in a large, shallow saucepan. Add the ginger, onion, garlic, chiles and cumin. Cook for about 5 minutes, until the onion is softened but not colored.

3 Stir the lentils, water and curry paste into the pan. Bring to a boil, cover and cook gently over low heat for 15–20 minutes, stirring occasionally, until the lentils are just tender and not yet broken up.

4 Stir in all but 2 tablespoons of the coconut cream. Bring to a boil and cook, uncovered, for another 15–20 minutes, until the mixture is thick and pulpy. Off the heat, stir in the lemon juice and cilantro leaves. Season to taste.

5 Heat a large frying pan and cook the almonds for one or two minutes on each side until golden brown. Stir about three-quarters of the toasted almonds into the dhal.

6 Transfer the dhal to a serving bowl; swirl in the remaining coconut cream. Sprinkle the reserved almonds on top and serve warm.

Hummus Bi Tahina

Blending chickpeas with garlic and oil creates a surprisingly creamy purée that is delicious as part of a Turkish-style mezze, or as a dip with vegetables. Leftovers make a good sandwich filler.

INGREDIENTS

Serves 4–6

¾ cup dried chickpeas

juice of 2 lemons

2 garlic cloves, sliced

2 tablespoons olive oil

pinch of cayenne pepper

⅔ cup tahini

salt and ground black pepper

extra olive oil and cayenne pepper, for sprinkling

flat-leaf parsley sprigs, to garnish

1 Put the chickpeas in a bowl with plenty of cold water and let to soak overnight.

2 Drain the chickpeas, place in a saucepan and cover with fresh water. Bring to a boil and boil rapidly for 10 minutes. Reduce the heat and simmer gently for about 1 hour, until soft. Drain in a colander.

3 Process the chickpeas in a food processor into a smooth purée. Add the lemon juice, garlic, olive oil, cayenne pepper and tahini paste and blend until creamy, scraping the mixture down from the sides of the bowl.

4 Season the purée with plenty of salt and ground black pepper and transfer to a serving dish. Sprinkle with a little olive oil and cayenne pepper, and serve garnished with a few parsley sprigs.

COOK'S TIP

For convenience, canned chickpeas can be used instead. Allow two 14-ounce cans and drain them thoroughly. Tahini can now be purchased at most good supermarkets or health food stores.

Baba Ganoush with Lebanese Flatbread

Baba Ganoush is a delectable eggplant dip from the Middle East. Tahini—a sesame seed paste with cumin—is the main flavoring, giving a subtle hint of spice.

INGREDIENTS

Serves 6

2 small eggplants

1 garlic clove, crushed

4 tablespoons tahini

¼ cup ground almonds

juice of ½ lemon

½ teaspoon ground cumin

2 tablespoons fresh mint leaves

2 tablespoons olive oil

salt and ground black pepper

For the flatbread

4 pita breads

3 tablespoons sesame seeds

3 tablespoons fresh thyme leaves

3 tablespoons poppy seeds

⅔ cup olive oil

1 Start by making the Lebanese flatbread. Split the pita breads through the middle and carefully open them out. Mix the sesame seeds, chopped thyme and poppy seeds in a mortar. Work them lightly with a pestle to release the flavor.

2 Stir in the olive oil. Spread the mixture on the cut sides of the pita bread. Broil until golden brown and crisp. When cool, break into pieces and set aside.

3 Broil the eggplants, turning them frequently, until the skin is blackened and blistered. Remove the peel, chop the flesh roughly and let drain in a colander.

4 Squeeze out as much liquid from the eggplant as possible. Place the flesh in a blender or food processor, then add the garlic, tahini, ground almonds, lemon juice and cumin, with salt to taste. Process into a smooth paste, then roughly chop half the mint and stir into the dip.

5 Spoon the paste into a bowl, sprinkle the remaining mint leaves on top and drizzle with the olive oil. Serve with the Lebanese flatbread.

Basil and Lemon Dip

This dip is based on fresh mayonnaise flavored with lemon juice and two types of basil. Serve with crispy potato wedges for a delicious treat.

INGREDIENTS

Serves 4

2 large egg yolks

1 tablespoon lemon juice

²⁄₃ cup olive oil

²⁄₃ cup sunflower oil

4 garlic cloves

handful of fresh green basil

handful of fresh opal basil

salt and ground black pepper

1 Place the egg yolks and lemon juice in a blender or food processor and process them briefly until lightly blended.

2 In a bowl, stir together the oils. With the machine running, pour in the oil very slowly, a little at a time.

3 Once half of the oil has been added, the remaining oil can be incorporated more quickly. Continue processing to form a thick, creamy mayonnaise.

4 Peel and crush the garlic cloves. Alternatively, place them on a cutting board and sprinkle with salt, then flatten them with the heel of a heavy-bladed knife and chop the flesh. Flatten the garlic again to make a coarse purée.

5 Tear both types of basil into small pieces and then stir into the mayonnaise along with the crushed garlic.

6 Add salt and pepper to taste, then transfer the dip to a serving dish. Cover and chill until ready to serve.

COOK'S TIP

Make sure all the ingredients are at room temperature before you start to help prevent the mixture from curdling.

Thai Tempeh Cakes with Dipping Sauce

Made from soy beans, tempeh is similar to tofu but has a nuttier taste. Here, it is combined with a fragrant blend of lemongrass, cilantro and ginger, and formed into small patties.

INGREDIENTS

Makes 8 cakes

1 lemongrass stalk, outer leaves removed, finely chopped

2 garlic cloves, finely chopped

2 scallions, finely chopped

2 shallots, finely chopped

2 chiles, seeded and finely chopped

1-inch piece fresh ginger, finely chopped

4 tablespoons chopped fresh cilantro, plus extra to garnish

2¼ cups tempeh, defrosted if frozen, sliced

1 tablespoon lime juice

1 teaspoon sugar

3 tablespoons all-purpose flour

1 large egg, lightly beaten

vegetable oil, for frying

salt and freshly ground black pepper

For the dipping sauce

3 tablespoons mirin

3 tablespoons white wine vinegar

2 scallions, finely sliced

1 tablespoon sugar

2 chiles, finely chopped

2 tablespoons chopped fresh cilantro

large pinch of salt

1 To make the dipping sauce, combine the mirin, vinegar, scallions, sugar, chiles, cilantro and salt in a small bowl and set aside.

2 Place the lemongrass, garlic, scallions, shallots, chiles, ginger and cilantro in a food processor or blender, then process into a coarse paste. Add the tempeh, lime juice and sugar, then blend until combined. Add the flour and egg, and season well. Process again until the mixture forms a coarse, sticky paste.

3 Take a heaping serving-spoonful of the tempeh paste mixture at a time and form into rounds with your hands. The mixture will be quite sticky.

4 Heat enough oil to cover the bottom of a large frying pan. Fry the tempeh cakes for 5–6 minutes, turning once, until golden. Drain on paper towels and serve warm with the dipping sauce, garnished with chopped fresh cilantro.

Guacamole

Avocados discolor quickly, so make this sauce just before serving. If you do need to keep it for any length of time, cover the surface of the sauce with plastic wrap and chill.

INGREDIENTS

Serves 6

2 large ripe avocados

2 red chiles, seeded

1 garlic clove

1 shallot

2 tablespoons olive oil, plus extra to serve

juice of 1 lemon

salt and ground black pepper

flat-leaf parsley, to garnish

1 Halve the avocados, remove the pit and scoop out the flesh into a large bowl.

2 Using a fork or potato masher, mash the avocado flesh until smooth.

3 Finely chop the chiles, garlic and shallot, then stir into the mashed avocado with the olive oil and lemon juice. Season to taste.

4 Spoon the mixture into a serving bowl. Drizzle over a little olive oil and scatter with a few flat-leaf parsley leaves. Serve immediately.

Quail's Eggs with Herbs and Dips

For al fresco eating or informal entertaining this platter of contrasting tastes and textures is delicious and certainly encourages a relaxed atmosphere. Choose the best seasonal vegetables and substitute for what is available.

INGREDIENTS

Serves 6

1 large Italian focaccia or 2–3 Indian
    parathas or other flatbread
high quality olive oil, plus extra to serve
1 large garlic clove, finely chopped
small handful of chopped fresh mixed
    herbs, such as cilantro, mint, parsley
    and oregano
18–24 quail's eggs
2 tablespoons homemade mayonnaise
2 tablespoons thick sour cream
1 teaspoon chopped capers
1 teaspoon finely chopped shallot
salt and ground black pepper
8 ounces fresh beets, cooked in water or
    cider, peeled and sliced
$\frac{1}{2}$ bunch scallions, trimmed and roughly
    chopped
4 tablespoons red onion or tamarind and
    date chutney
coarse sea salt and mixed ground
    peppercorns, to serve

1 Preheat the oven to 375°F. Brush the focaccia or flatbread liberally with oil, sprinkle with garlic, your choice of herbs and seasoning and bake for 10–15 minutes or until golden. Keep warm.

2 Put the quail's eggs into a saucepan of cold water, bring to a boil and boil for 5 minutes. Arrange in a serving dish. Peel the eggs if you wish, or leave guests to do their own.

3 To make the dip, combine the mayonnaise, sour cream, capers, shallot and seasoning.

4 To serve, cut the bread into wedges and serve with dishes of the quail's eggs, mayonnaise dip, beets, scallions and chutney. Serve with tiny bowls of the coarse salt, ground peppercorns and olive oil for dipping.

COOK'S TIP

If you don't have time to make your own mayonnaise use the best store-bought variety available. You will probably find that you need to add less seasoning to it.

Tzatziki

Serve this classic Greek dip with toasted small pita breads.

INGREDIENTS

Serves 4

1 mini cucumber

4 scallions

1 garlic clove

scant 1 cup plain yogurt

3 tablespoons chopped fresh mint

fresh mint sprig, to garnish (optional)

salt and ground black pepper

1 Trim the ends from the mini cucumber, then cut it into ¼-inch dice.

2 Trim the scallions and garlic, then chop both very finely.

COOK'S TIP

Using strained, plain yogurt for this dip will enhance this recipe, giving it a more deliciously rich and creamy texture.

3 In a glass bowl, beat the yogurt until completely smooth, if necessary, then gently stir in the chopped cucumber, onions, garlic and mint.

4 Add salt and plenty of freshly ground black pepper to taste. Transfer the mixture to a serving bowl. Chill until ready to serve; garnish with mint, if desired.

Parmesan Fish Goujons

Use this batter, with or without the cheese, whenever you feel brave enough to fry fish. This is light and crisp, just like authentic British fish-and-chips.

INGREDIENTS

Serves 4

13 ounces plaice or sole fillets, or thicker
    fish such as cod or haddock
a little all-purpose flour
oil, for deep-frying
salt and ground black pepper
dill sprigs, to garnish

For the tartar sauce
4 tablespoons sour cream
4 tablespoons mayonnaise
½ teaspoon grated lemon zest
2 tablespoons chopped gherkins or capers
1 tablespoon chopped mixed fresh herbs,
    or 1 teaspoon dried

For the batter
¾ cup all-purpose flour
¼ cup grated Parmesan cheese
1 teaspoon baking soda
1 egg, separated
⅔ cup milk

1 To make the cream sauce, mix the sour cream, mayonnaise, lemon zest, gherkins or capers, herbs and seasoning, then place in the refrigerator to chill.

2 To make the batter, sift the flour into a bowl. Mix in the other dry ingredients and some salt, and then whisk in the egg yolk and milk to give a thick yet smooth batter. Then gradually whisk in 6 tablespoons water. Season and place in the refrigerator to chill.

3 Skin the fish and cut into thin strips of similar length. Season the flour and then dip the fish lightly in the flour.

4 Heat at least 2 inches oil in a large pan with a lid. Whisk the egg white until stiff and gently fold into the batter until just blended.

5 Dip the floured fish into the batter, drain off any excess and then drop gently into the hot fat.

6 Cook the fish in batches so that the goujons don't stick to one another for only 3–4 minutes, turning once. When the batter is golden and crisp, remove the fish with a slotted spoon. Place on paper towels on a plate and keep warm in a low oven while cooking the remaining goujons.

7 Serve hot garnished with sprigs of dill and accompanied by the sauce.

Jumbo Shrimp in Crispy Batter

Serve these delightfully crispy shrimp with an Asian-style dipping sauce, or offer a simple tomato sauce or lemon wedges for squeezing.

INGREDIENTS

Serves 4

½ cup water

1 egg

1 cup all-purpose flour

1 teaspoon cayenne pepper

12 jumbo shrimp, unpeeled

vegetable oil, for deep-frying

flat-leaf parsley, to garnish

lemon wedges, to serve

For the dipping sauce

2 tablespoons soy sauce

2 tablespoons dry sherry

2 teaspoons honey

3 To make the dipping sauce, stir together the soy sauce, dry sherry and honey in a small bowl until well combined.

4 Heat the oil in a large saucepan or deep-fryer, until a cube of stale bread tossed in browns in 1 minute.

5 Holding the shrimp by their tails, dip them into the batter, one at a time, shaking off any excess. Drop the shrimp carefully into the oil and fry for 2–3 minutes, until crisp and golden brown. Drain on paper towels and serve with the dipping sauce and lemon wedges, garnished with parsley.

1 In a large bowl, whisk the water with the egg. Add the flour and cayenne, and whisk until smooth.

2 Carefully peel the shrimp, leaving just the tail sections intact. Make a shallow cut down the back of each shrimp, then pull out and discard the dark intestinal tract.

COOK'S TIP

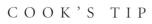

Use leftover batter to coat thin strips of sweet potato, beets, carrot or bell pepper, then deep-fry until golden.

Duck Wontons with Spicy Mango Sauce

These Chinese-style wontons are easy to make using ready-cooked smoked duck or chicken, or even leftovers from the Sunday roast.

Makes about 40

1 tablespoon light soy sauce

1 teaspoon sesame oil

2 scallions, finely chopped

grated zest of ½ orange

1 teaspoon brown sugar

1½ cups chopped smoked duck

about 40 small wonton wrappers

1 tablespoon vegetable oil

whole fresh chives, to garnish (optional)

For the mango sauce

2 tablespoons vegetable oil

1 teaspoon ground cumin

½ teaspoon ground cardamom

¼ teaspoon ground cinnamon

1 cup mango purée (about 1 large mango)

1 tablespoon honey

½ teaspoon Chinese chili sauce (or to taste)

1 tablespoon cider vinegar

snipped fresh chives, to garnish

2 Stir in the mango purée, honey, chili sauce and vinegar. Remove from heat and let cool. Pour into a bowl and cover until ready to serve.

3 Prepare the wonton filling. In a large bowl, combine the soy sauce, sesame oil, scallions, orange zest and brown sugar until well blended. Add the duck and toss to coat well.

5 Preheat the oven to 375°C. Line a large baking sheet with aluminum foil and brush lightly with oil. Arrange the wontons on the baking sheet and bake for 10–12 minutes, until crisp and golden. Serve with the mango sauce garnished with snipped fresh chives. If desired, tie each wonton with a fresh chive.

1 First prepare the sauce. In a medium saucepan, heat the oil over medium-low heat. Add the ground cumin, cardamom and cinnamon and cook for about 3 minutes, stirring constantly.

4 Place a teaspoonful of the duck mixture in the center of each wonton wrapper. Brush the edges with water and then draw them up to the center, twisting to seal and forming a pouch shape.

COOK'S TIP

Wonton wrappers, available at some large supermarkets and Asian food stores, are sold in 1 pound packages and can be stored in the freezer almost indefinitely. Remove as many as you need, keeping the rest frozen.

Pork and Peanut Wontons with Plum Sauce

These crispy filled wontons are delicious served with a sweet plum sauce. The wontons can be filled and set aside for up to 8 hours before they are cooked.

INGREDIENTS

Makes 40–50 wontons

1½ cups ground pork or 6 ounces pork
    sausages, skinned
2 scallions, finely chopped
2 tablespoons peanut butter
2 teaspoons oyster sauce (optional)
40–50 wonton skins
2 tablespoons flour paste
vegetable oil, for deep-frying
salt and ground black pepper
lettuces and radishes, to garnish

For the plum sauce
generous ¾ cup dark plum jam
1 tablespoon rice or white wine vinegar
1 tablespoon dark soy sauce
½ teaspoon chili sauce

1 Combine the ground pork or skinned sausages, scallions, peanut butter, oyster sauce, if using, and seasoning, and then set aside.

2 For the plum sauce, combine the plum jam, vinegar, soy and chili sauces in a serving bowl and set aside.

3 To fill the wonton skins, place 8 wrappers at a time on a work surface, moisten the edges with the flour paste and place ½ teaspoon of the filling on each one. Fold in half, corner to corner, and twist.

4 Fill a wok or deep frying pan one-third with vegetable oil and heat to 385°F. Have ready a wire strainer or frying basket and a tray lined with paper towels. Drop the wontons, 8 at a time, into the hot fat and fry until golden all over, for 1–2 minutes. Lift out on to the paper-lined tray and sprinkle with fine salt. Serve with the plum sauce garnished with lettuce and radishes.

Pork Balls with a Minted Peanut Sauce

This recipe is equally delicious made with chicken breasts.

INGREDIENTS

Serves 4–6

10 ounces leg of pork, trimmed and diced

½-inch piece fresh ginger, peeled and grated

1 garlic clove, crushed

2 teaspoons sesame oil

1 tablespoon medium-dry sherry

1 tablespoon soy sauce

1 teaspoon sugar

1 egg white

½ teaspoon salt

pinch of white pepper

scant 1¾ cups long grain rice, washed and cooked for 15 minutes

2 ounces ham, diced

1 iceberg lettuce, to serve

For the peanut sauce

1 tablespoon creamed coconut

⅓ cup boiling water

2 tablespoons smooth peanut butter

juice of 1 lime

1 red chile, seeded and finely chopped

1 garlic clove, crushed

1 tablespoon chopped fresh mint

1 tablespoon chopped fresh cilantro

1 tablespoon fish sauce (optional)

1 Place the pork, ginger and garlic in a food processor; process for 2–3 minutes, until smooth. Add the sesame oil, sherry, soy sauce and sugar and blend with the pork mixture. Finally, add the egg white, salt and white pepper.

2 Spread the cooked rice and ham in a shallow dish. Using wet hands, shape the pork mixture into thumb-size balls. Roll in the rice to coat and pierce each ball with a bamboo skewer.

3 To make the peanut sauce, put the creamed coconut in a measuring cup and cover with the boiling water. Place the peanut butter in another bowl with the lime juice, chile, garlic, mint and cilantro. Combine evenly, then add the creamed coconut and season with the fish sauce if using.

4 Place the pork balls in a bamboo steamer then steam over a saucepan of boiling water for 8–10 minutes. Arrange the pork balls on lettuce leaves on a plate with the sauce to one side.

Chicken Saté with Peanut Sauce

These skewers of marinated chicken can be prepared in advance and served at room temperature. Beef, pork or even lamb fillet can be used instead of chicken, if you prefer.

INGREDIENTS

Makes about 24

1 pound boneless, skinless chicken breasts

oil, for brushing

sesame seeds, for sprinkling

red bell pepper strips, to garnish

For the marinade

6 tablespoons vegetable oil

4 tablespoons tamari or light soy sauce

4 tablespoons fresh lime juice

1-inch piece fresh ginger,
    peeled and chopped

3–4 garlic cloves

2 tablespoons light brown sugar

1 teaspoon Chinese-style chili sauce or
    1 small red chile pepper, seeded
    and chopped

2 tablespoons chopped cilantro

For the peanut sauce

2 tablespoon smooth peanut butter

2 tablespoon soy sauce

1 tablespoon sesame or vegetable oil

2 scallions, chopped

2 garlic cloves

1–2 tablespoons fresh lime or lemon juice

1 tablespoon brown sugar

COOK'S TIP

When using metal skewers, look for flat ones that prevent the food from spinning around. If using wooden skewers, be sure to soak them in cold water for at least 30 minutes, to prevent them from burning.

1 Prepare the marinade. Place all the marinade ingredients in a food processor or blender and process until smooth and well blended, scraping down the sides of the bowl once. Pour into a shallow dish and set aside.

2 Into the same food processor or blender, put all the peanut sauce ingredients and process until well blended. If the sauce is too thick, add a little water and process again. Pour into a small bowl and cover until ready to serve.

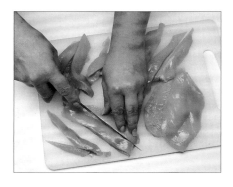

3 Slice the chicken breasts into thin strips, then cut the strips into ¾-inch pieces.

4 Add the chicken pieces to the marinade in the dish. Toss well to coat, cover and marinate for 3–4 hours in a cool place or overnight in the refrigerator.

5 Preheat the broiler. Line a baking sheet with aluminum foil and brush lightly with oil. Thread 2–3 pieces of marinated chicken onto skewers and sprinkle with the sesame seeds. Broil for 4–5 minutes until golden, turning once. Serve with the peanut sauce, and a garnish of red bell pepper strips.

Jumbo Shrimp with Spicy Dip

The spicy dip served with this dish is equally good made from peanuts instead of cashews. Vegetarians can enjoy this, too, if you make it with vegetables or tofu cubes.

INGREDIENTS

Serves 4–6

24 jumbo shrimp, unpeeled
juice of ½ lemon
1 teaspoon paprika
1 bay leaf
1 thyme sprig
vegetable oil, for brushing
salt and ground black pepper

For the spicy dip

1 onion, chopped
4 canned plum tomatoes, plus
   4 tablespoons of the juice
½ green bell pepper, seeded and chopped
1 garlic clove, crushed
1 tablespoon cashews
1 tablespoon soy sauce
1 tablespoon dry, shredded coconut

1 Peel the shrimp, leaving the tails on. Place in a shallow dish and sprinkle with the lemon juice, paprika and seasoning. Cover and chill in the refrigerator.

2 Put the shells in a saucepan with the bay leaf and thyme, cover with water, and bring to a boil. Simmer for 30 minutes; strain the stock into a measuring pitcher. Add water, if necessary, to make 1¼ cups.

3 To make the spicy dip, place all the ingredients in a blender or food processor and process until the mixture is smooth.

4 Pour into a saucepan with the shrimp stock and simmer over medium heat for 30 minutes, until the sauce is fairly thick.

5 Preheat the broiler. Thread the shrimp onto small skewers, then brush the shrimp on both sides with a little oil and broil under low heat until cooked, turning once. Serve with the dip.

COOK'S TIP

∽

If unshelled shrimp are not available, use cooked shrimp instead. Just broil them for a short time, until they are completely heated through.

Beef Saté with a Hot Mango Dip

Strips of tender beef are flavored with a delicious spicy marinade before being broiled, then served with a fruit dip.

Makes 12 skewers

1 pound sirloin steak,
   ³⁄₄-inch thick, trimmed

For the marinade

1 tablespoon coriander seeds

1 teaspoon cumin seeds

¹⁄₃ cup raw cashews

1 tablespoon vegetable oil

2 shallots, or 1 small onion, finely chopped

½-inch piece fresh ginger, peeled and
   finely chopped

1 garlic clove, crushed

2 tablespoons tamarind sauce

2 tablespoons dark soy sauce

2 teaspoons sugar

1 teaspoon rice or white wine vinegar

For the mango dip

1 ripe mango

1–2 small red chiles, seeded and
   finely chopped

1 tablespoon fish sauce

juice of 1 lime

2 teaspoons sugar

¼ teaspoon salt

2 tablespoons chopped fresh cilantro

1 Soak 12 bamboo skewers for 30 minutes. Slice the beef into long narrow strips and thread, zigzag-style, onto the skewers. Lay on a flat plate and set aside.

2 For the marinade, dry-fry the seeds and nuts in a large wok until evenly brown. Transfer to a mortar with a rough surface and crush finely with the pestle. Add the oil, shallots or onion, ginger, garlic, tamarind and soy sauces, sugar and white wine vinegar.

3 Spread this marinade on the beef and let marinate for up to 8 hours. Cook the beef under a medium broiler or on a grill for 6–8 minutes, turning to ensure an even color. Meanwhile, make the mango dip.

4 Cut off the skin and remove the pit from the mango. Process the mango flesh with the chiles, fish sauce, lime juice, sugar and salt until smooth, then add the cilantro.

Skewered Lamb with Red Onion Salsa

This summery tapas dish is ideal for outdoor eating, although, if the weather fails, the skewers can be broiled rather than grilled. The simple salsa makes a refreshing accompaniment—make sure that you use a mild-flavored red onion that is fresh and crisp, and a tomato which is ripe and full of flavor.

INGREDIENTS

Serves 4

8 ounces lean lamb, cubed

½ teaspoon ground cumin

1 teaspoon paprika

1 tablespoon olive oil

salt and ground black pepper

For the salsa

1 red onion, very thinly sliced

1 large tomato, seeded and chopped

1 tablespoon red wine vinegar

3–4 fresh basil or mint leaves,
   coarsely torn

small mint leaves, to garnish

1 Place the lamb in a bowl with the cumin, paprika, olive oil and plenty of salt and pepper. Toss well until the lamb is coated with spices.

2 Cover the bowl with plastic wrap and set aside in a cool place for a few hours or in the refrigerator overnight, so that the lamb absorbs the flavors.

3 Spear the lamb cubes on four small skewers—if using wooden skewers, soak first in cold water for 30 minutes to prevent them from burning.

4 To make the salsa, put the sliced onion, tomato, red wine vinegar and basil or mint leaves in a small bowl and stir together until thoroughly blended. Season to taste with salt, garnish with mint, then set aside while you cook the lamb skewers.

5 Cook on the grill or under a preheated broiler for 5–10 minutes, turning frequently, until the lamb is well browned but still slightly pink in the center. Serve hot, with the salsa.

Five-spice Rib-sticker

Choose the meatiest spare ribs you can, to make these a real success.

INGREDIENTS

Serves 8

2¼ pounds pork spare ribs

2 teaspoons Chinese five-spice powder

2 garlic cloves, crushed

1 tablespoon grated fresh ginger

½ teaspoon chili sauce

4 tablespoons dark brown sugar

1 tablespoon sunflower oil

4 scallions

3 Cook the spare ribs under a preheated medium-hot broiler turning frequently, for 30–40 minutes. Brush the ribs occasionally with the remaining marinade.

4 While the ribs are cooking, finely slice the scallions—on the diagonal. To serve, place the ribs on a serving plate and sprinkle the scallions on top.

1 If the spare ribs are still attached together, cut between them to separate them (or ask your butcher to do this). Place the spare ribs in a large bowl.

2 Combine all the remaining ingredients, except the scallions, and pour onto the ribs. Toss well to coat evenly. Cover the bowl and let marinate in the refrigerator overnight.

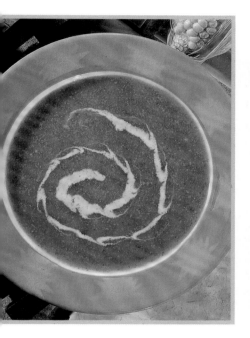  

SOUPS

Cold Cucumber and Yogurt Soup

This refreshing cold soup uses the classic combination of cucumber and yogurt, with the added flavor of garlic and pleasant crunch of walnuts.

INGREDIENTS

Serves 5–6

1 cucumber

4 garlic cloves

½ teaspoon salt

¾ cup walnut pieces

1½ ounces day-old bread, torn into pieces

2 tablespoons walnut or sunflower oil

1⅔ cups sheep's or cow's milk yogurt

½ cup cold water or chilled still mineral water

1–2 teaspoons lemon juice

scant ½ cup walnuts, chopped, to garnish

olive oil, for drizzling

dill sprigs, to garnish

3 When the mixture is smooth, add the walnut or sunflower oil slowly and combine well.

4 Transfer the walnut and bread mixture to a large bowl, then beat in the cow's or sheep's milk yogurt and the diced cucumber.

5 Add the cold water or mineral water and lemon juice to taste.

6 Pour the soup into chilled soup bowls to serve. Garnish with the chopped walnuts, a little olive oil drizzled on the nuts and sprigs of dill.

1 Cut the cucumber into two and peel one half of it. Dice the cucumber flesh and set aside.

2 Using a large mortar and pestle, crush the garlic and salt together well, then add the walnuts and bread.

COOK'S TIP

If you prefer your soup smooth, purée it in a food processor or blender before serving.

Chilled Tomato and Sweet Bell Pepper Soup

This recipe was inspired by the Spanish gazpacho, the difference being that this soup is cooked first, and then chilled.

INGREDIENTS

Serves 4

2 red bell peppers, halved, cored and seeded

3 tablespoons olive oil

1 onion, finely chopped

2 garlic cloves, crushed

1½ pounds ripe well-flavored tomatoes

⅔ cup red wine

2½ cups chicken stock

salt and ground black pepper

snipped fresh chives, to garnish

For the croûtons

2 slices white bread, crusts removed

4 tablespoons olive oil

1 Cut each red bell pepper half into quarters. Place skin side up on a broiler pan and cook until the skins are charred. Transfer to a bowl and cover with a plate or pop into a plastic bag and seal.

2 Heat the oil in a large pan. Add the onion and garlic and cook gently until soft. Meanwhile, remove the skin from the peppers and roughly chop the flesh. Cut the tomatoes into chunks.

3 Add the peppers and tomatoes to the pan, then cover and cook gently for 10 minutes. Add the wine and cook for another 5 minutes, then add the stock and salt and pepper and continue to simmer for 20 minutes.

4 To make the croûtons, cut the bread into cubes. Heat the oil in a small frying pan, add the bread and fry until golden. Drain on paper towels and store in an airtight box.

5 Process the soup in a blender or food processor until smooth. Pour into a clean glass or ceramic bowl and let cool thoroughly before chilling in the refrigerator for at least 3 hours. When the soup is cold, season to taste.

6 Serve the soup in bowls, topped with the croûtons and garnished with snipped chives.

Chilled Asparagus Soup

This soup provides a delightful way to enjoy a favorite seasonal vegetable. Choose bright, crisp-looking asparagus with firm, slender stalks.

INGREDIENTS

Serves 6

2 pounds fresh asparagus

4 tablespoons butter or olive oil

1½ cups sliced leeks or scallions

3 tablespoons all-purpose flour

6¼ cups chicken stock or water

½ cup light cream or plain yogurt

salt and ground black pepper

1 tablespoon minced fresh tarragon or chervil

3 Heat the butter or olive oil in a heavy saucepan. Add the leeks or scallions and cook over low heat until softened, 5–8 minutes. Stir in the chopped asparagus stalks, cover and cook for another 6–8 minutes.

4 Add the flour and stir well to blend. Cook for 3–4 minutes, uncovered, stirring occasionally.

5 Add the stock or water and bring to a boil, stirring frequently, then reduce the heat and simmer for 30 minutes. Season with salt and pepper.

6 Purée the soup in a food processor or blender. If necessary, strain it to remove any coarse fibers. Stir in the asparagus tips, most of the cream or yogurt, and the herbs. Cool, then chill well. Stir thoroughly before serving, and check the seasoning. Garnish with the remaining cream or yogurt.

1 Cut the top 2½ inches off the asparagus spears. Blanch these tips in boiling water until they are just tender, 5–6 minutes. Drain. Cut each tip into 2 or 3 pieces, and set aside.

2 Trim the ends of the stalks, removing any brown or woody parts. Chop the asparagus stalks into ½-inch pieces.

COOK'S TIP

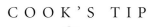

Chilled soups can require extra seasoning, so remember to check the taste just before you serve.

Gazpacho with Avocado Salsa

Tomatoes, cucumber and bell peppers form the basis of this classic, chilled soup. Add a spoonful of chunky, fresh avocado salsa and croûtons for a delicious summer soup. This is quite a substantial soup, so follow with a light main course, such as grilled fish or chicken.

INGREDIENTS

Serves 4–6

2 slices day-old bread

2½ cups chilled water

2¼ pounds tomatoes

1 cucumber

1 red bell pepper, seeded and chopped

1 green chile, seeded and chopped

2 garlic cloves, chopped

2 tablespoons extra virgin olive oil

juice of 1 lime and 1 lemon

few drops of Tabasco sauce

salt and ground black pepper

handful of fresh basil, to garnish

8–12 ice cubes, to serve

For the croûtons

2–3 slices day-old bread, crusts removed

1 garlic clove, halved

1–2 tablespoons olive oil

For the avocado salsa

1 ripe avocado

1 teaspoon lemon juice

1-inch piece cucumber, diced

½ red chile, finely chopped

1 Make the soup first. In a shallow bowl, soak the day-old bread in ⅔ cup water for 5 minutes.

COOK'S TIP
〜

For a superior flavor choose Haas avocados with the rough-textured, almost black skins.

2 Meanwhile, place the tomatoes in a heatproof bowl; cover with boiling water. Leave for 30 seconds, then peel, seed and chop the flesh.

3 Thinly peel the cucumber, cut in half lengthwise and scoop out the seeds with a teaspoon. Discard the seeds and chop the flesh.

4 Place the bread, tomatoes, cucumber, red bell pepper, chile, garlic, oil, citrus juices, Tabasco and a scant 2 cups chilled water in a food processor or blender. Blend until mixed but still chunky. Season and chill well.

5 To make the croûtons, rub the slices of bread with the cut surface of the garlic clove. Cut the bread into cubes and place in a plastic bag with the olive oil. Seal the bag and shake until the bread cubes are coated with the oil. Heat a large nonstick frying pan and fry the croûtons over medium heat until crisp and golden.

6 Just before serving make the avocado salsa. Halve the avocado, remove the pit, then peel and dice the flesh. Toss the avocado in the lemon juice to prevent it from browning, then mix with the cucumber and chile.

7 Ladle the soup into bowls, add the ice cubes, and top with a spoonful of avocado salsa. Garnish with the basil and pass the croûtons separately.

Chilled Shrimp and Cucumber Soup

If you've never served a chilled soup before, this is the one to try first. Delicious and light, it's the perfect way to celebrate summer.

INGREDIENTS

Serves 4

2 tablespoons butter

2 shallots, finely chopped

2 garlic cloves, crushed

1 cucumber, peeled, seeded and diced

1¼ cups milk

8 ounces cooked peeled shrimp

1 tablespoon each finely chopped fresh
mint, dill, chives and chervil

1¼ cups whipping cream

salt and ground white pepper

For the garnish

2 tablespoons crème fraîche
or sour cream (optional)

4 large, cooked shrimp, peeled with
tail intact

fresh chives and dill

1 Melt the butter in a saucepan and cook the shallots and garlic over low heat until soft but not colored. Add the cucumber and cook the vegetables gently, stirring frequently, until tender.

2 Stir in the milk, bring almost to a boil, then lower the heat and simmer for 5 minutes. Put the soup into a blender or food processor and purée until very smooth. Season to taste with salt and ground white pepper.

3 Pour the soup into a bowl and set aside to cool. When cool, stir in the shrimp, chopped herbs and the whipping cream. Cover, transfer to the refrigerator and chill for at least 2 hours.

4 To serve, ladle the soup into four individual bowls and top each portion with a dollop of crème fraîche or sour cream, if using. Place a shrimp over the edge of each dish. Garnish with the chives and dill.

COOK'S TIP

For a change try fresh or canned crabmeat, or cooked, flaked salmon fillet.

Hot-and-sour Soup

This light and invigorating soup originates from Thailand. It is traditionally served at the beginning of a formal Thai meal to stimulate the appetite.

INGREDIENTS

Serves 4

2 carrots

3¾ cups vegetable stock

2 Thai chiles, seeded and finely sliced

2 lemongrass stalks, outer leaves removed and each stalk cut into 3 pieces

4 kaffir lime leaves

2 garlic cloves, finely chopped

4 scallions, finely sliced

1 teaspoon sugar

juice of 1 lime

3 tablespoons chopped fresh cilantro

salt, to taste

1 cup Japanese tofu, sliced

1 To make carrot flowers, cut each carrot in half crosswise, then, using a sharp knife, cut four V-shaped channels lengthwise. Slice the carrots into thin rounds and set aside.

2 Pour the vegetable stock into a large saucepan. Reserve ½ teaspoon of the chiles and add the rest to the pan with the lemongrass, lime leaves, garlic and half the scallions. Bring to a boil, then reduce the heat and simmer for 20 minutes. Strain the stock and discard the flavorings.

3 Return the stock to the pan, add the reserved chilies and scallions, the sugar, lime juice, cilantro and salt to taste.

4 Simmer for 5 minutes, then add the carrot flowers and tofu slices, and cook the soup for another 2 minutes, until the carrot is just tender. Serve hot.

COOK'S TIP

Kaffir lime leaves have a distinctive citrus flavor. The fresh leaves can be bought at Asian stores, and some supermarkets now sell them dried.

Corn Soup

This is a simple to make yet very flavorful soup. It is sometimes made with sour cream and cream cheese. Poblano chilies may be added, but these are rather difficult to locate outside Mexico. However, you may be able to find them canned at some of the larger supermarkets and delicatessens.

INGREDIENTS

Serves 4

2 tablespoons corn oil

1 onion, finely chopped

1 red bell pepper, seeded and chopped

1 pound corn kernels, thawed if frozen

3 cups chicken stock

1 cup light cream

salt and ground black pepper

½ red bell pepper, seeded and finely diced, to garnish

1 Heat the oil in a frying pan and sauté the onion and red pepper for about 5 minutes, until soft. Add the corn and sauté for 2 minutes.

2 Carefully put the contents of the pan in a food processor or blender. Process until the mixture is smooth, scraping down the sides and adding a little of the stock, if necessary.

3 Put the mixture in a clean saucepan and stir in the stock. Season to taste with salt and pepper, bring to a simmer and cook for 5 minutes.

4 Gently stir in the cream. Serve the soup hot or chilled, with the diced red pepper sprinkled on top. If serving hot, reheat gently after adding the cream, but do not let the soup boil.

Zucchini Soup

This soup is so simple—in terms of ingredients and preparation. It would provide an elegant start to a dinner party.

INGREDIENTS

Serves 4

2 tablespoons butter

1 onion, finely chopped

1 pound young zucchini, trimmed and chopped

3 cups chicken stock

½ cup light cream, plus extra to serve

salt and ground black pepper

1 Melt the butter in a saucepan and sauté the onion until it is soft. Add the zucchini and cook, stirring, for about 1–2 minutes.

2 Add the chicken stock. Bring to a boil over medium heat and then simmer for about 5 minutes or until the zucchini are just tender.

> ### COOK'S TIP
> ❧
> Always use the smallest zucchini available, as these have the best flavor.

3 Strain the stock into a clean saucepan, saving the vegetable solids in the sieve. Purée the solids in the food processor and add to the pan. Season to taste with salt and pepper.

4 Stir the cream into the soup and heat through very gently without letting it boil. Serve hot with a little extra cream swirled in.

Pear and Watercress Soup

The pears in the soup are complemented beautifully by Stilton croûtons. Their flavors make them natural partners.

INGREDIENTS

Serves 6

1 bunch watercress

4 pears, sliced

3¾ cups chicken stock,
    preferably homemade

½ cup heavy cream

juice of 1 lime

salt and ground black pepper

For the croûtons

2 tablespoons butter

1 tablespoon olive oil

3 cups cubed stale bread

1 cup chopped Stilton

1 Set aside about a third of the watercress leaves. Place the rest of the leaves and stalks in a pan with the pears, stock and a little seasoning. Simmer for about 15–20 minutes. Reserving some watercress leaves for garnishing, add the rest of the leaves and then purée in a blender or food processor until smooth.

2 Put the mixture in a bowl and stir in the cream and the lime juice to mix the flavors thoroughly. Season again to taste. Pour all the soup back into a pan and reheat, stirring gently until warmed through.

3 To make the croûtons, melt the butter and oil and fry the bread cubes until golden brown. Drain on paper towels. Put the cheese on top and heat under a hot broiler until bubbling. Reheat the soup and pour into bowls. Divide the croûtons and the reserved watercress leaves between the bowls and serve immediately.

Baby Carrot and Fennel Soup

Sweet tender carrots find their moment of glory in this delicately spiced soup. Fennel provides a very subtle aniseed flavor that does not overpower the carrots.

INGREDIENTS

Serves 4

4 tablespoons butter

1 small bunch scallions, chopped

5-ounce fennel bulb, chopped

1 celery stalk, chopped

1 pound new carrots, grated

½ teaspoon ground cumin

5 ounces new potatoes, peeled and diced

5 cups chicken or vegetable stock

4 tablespoons heavy cream

salt and ground black pepper

4 tablespoons chopped fresh parsley, to garnish

1 Melt the butter in a large saucepan and add the scallions, fennel, celery, carrots and cumin. Cover and cook for about 5 minutes or until soft.

COOK'S TIP

For convenience, you can freeze the soup in portions before adding the cream, seasoning and parsley.

2 Add the diced potatoes and chicken or vegetable stock, and simmer the mixture for another 10 minutes.

3 Liquidize the soup in the pan with a hand-held blender. Stir in the cream and season to taste. Serve in individual soup bowls and garnish with chopped parsley.

Spanish Garlic Soup

This is a simple and satisfying soup, made with one of the most popular ingredients in the Mediterranean region—garlic!

INGREDIENTS

Serves 4

2 tablespoons olive oil

4 large garlic cloves, peeled

4 slices French bread, ¼-inch thick

1 tablespoon paprika

4 cups beef stock

¼ teaspoon ground cumin

pinch of saffron threads

4 eggs

salt and ground black pepper

chopped fresh parsley, to garnish

1 Preheat the oven to 450°F. Heat the oil in a large pan. Add the whole garlic cloves and cook until golden. Remove and set aside. Fry the bread in the oil until golden, then set aside.

COOK'S TIP

Use homemade beef stock for the best flavor or buy prepared stock at your supermarket—you'll find it in the refrigerated section. Never use bouillon cubes, as they contain too much salt.

2 Add the paprika to the pan, and fry for a few seconds, stirring. Stir in the beef stock, the cumin and saffron, then add the reserved fried garlic, crushing the cloves with the back of a wooden spoon. Season with salt and ground black pepper then cook for about 5 minutes.

3 Ladle the soup into four ovenproof bowls and gently break an egg into each one. Place the slices of fried French bread on top of the eggs and place in the oven for 3–4 minutes or until the eggs are set. Sprinkle with chopped fresh parsley and serve immediately.

Fresh Tomato Soup

Intensely flavored sun-ripened tomatoes need little embellishment in this fresh-tasting soup. If you buy them at the supermarket, choose the juiciest looking ones and add the amount of sugar and vinegar necessary, depending on their natural sweetness. On a hot day this Italian soup is also delicious chilled.

Serves 6

3–3½ pounds ripe tomatoes

1⅔ cups chicken or vegetable stock

3 tablespoons sun-dried tomato paste

2–3 tablespoons balsamic vinegar

2–3 teaspoons sugar

small handful of basil leaves

salt and ground black pepper

basil leaves, to garnish

toasted cheese croûtes and crème fraîche,
     to serve

1 Plunge the tomatoes into boiling water for 30 seconds, then refresh in cold water. Peel off the skins and quarter the tomatoes. Put them in a large saucepan and pour over the chicken or vegetable stock. Bring just to a boil, reduce the heat, cover and simmer the mixture gently for 10 minutes, until the tomatoes are pulpy.

2 Stir in the tomato paste, vinegar, sugar and basil. Season with salt and pepper, then cook gently, stirring, for 2 minutes. Process the soup in a blender or food processor, then return to the pan and reheat gently. Serve in bowls topped with one or two toasted cheese croûtes and a spoonful of crème fraîche, garnished with basil leaves.

Avocado Soup

To add a subtle garlic flavor, rub the cut side of a garlic clove around the soup bowls before adding the soup.

Serves 4

2 large ripe avocados

4 cups chicken stock

1 cup light cream

salt and ground white pepper

1 tablespoon finely chopped cilantro, to garnish (optional)

3 Season to taste with salt and pepper. Serve immediately, sprinkled with the cilantro, if using. The soup may be served chilled, if desired.

2 Heat the chicken stock with the cream in a saucepan. When the mixture is hot, but not boiling, whisk it into the puréed avocado.

1 Cut the avocados in half, remove the pits and mash the flesh (see Cook's Tip). Put the flesh into a sieve and with a wooden spoon, press it through into a warmed bowl.

COOK'S TIP

The easiest way to mash the avocados is to hold each pitted half in turn in the palm of one hand and mash the flesh in the shell with a fork, before scooping it into the bowl. This keeps the avocado from slithering around when it is being mashed.

Vermicelli Soup

The inclusion of fresh cilantro adds a piquancy to this soup and complements the tomato flavor.

INGREDIENTS

Serves 4

2 tablespoons olive or corn oil

2 ounces vermicelli

1 onion, roughly chopped

1 garlic clove, chopped

1 pound tomatoes, peeled, seeded and
   roughly chopped

4 cups chicken stock

1/4 teaspoon sugar

1 tablespoon finely chopped cilantro

salt and ground black pepper

chopped fresh cilantro, to garnish

1/4 cup freshly grated Parmesan cheese, to
   serve

1 Heat the oil in a frying pan and sauté the vermicelli over medium heat, until golden brown. Be careful not to let the strands burn. Remove the vermicelli with a slotted spoon or tongs and drain on paper towels.

COOK'S TIP

Vermicelli burns very easily, so move it around continuously in the frying pan with a wooden spoon and remove it from the heat as soon as it turns a golden brown color.

2 Purée the onion, garlic and tomatoes in a food processor or blender until smooth. Return the frying pan to the heat. When the oil is hot again, add the purée to the pan. Cook, stirring constantly to prevent sticking, for about 5 minutes or until thick.

3 Transfer the purée to a saucepan. Add the vermicelli and pour in the stock. Season with sugar, salt and pepper. Stir in the cilantro, bring to a boil, then lower the heat, cover the pan and simmer the soup gently until the vermicelli is tender.

4 Serve in warmed soup bowls, sprinkle with chopped fresh cilantro and pass the grated Parmesan cheese separately.

Wild Mushroom Soup

Wild mushrooms are expensive, but dried porcini have an intense flavor, so only a small amount is needed. The beef stock may seem unusual in a vegetable soup, but it helps to strengthen the earthy flavor of the mushrooms.

INGREDIENTS

Serves 4

1 cup dried porcini mushrooms

2 tablespoons olive oil

1 tablespoon butter

2 leeks, thinly sliced

2 shallots, roughly chopped

1 garlic clove, roughly chopped

3 cups fresh wild mushrooms

about 5 cups beef stock

½ teaspoon dried thyme

⅔ cup heavy cream

salt and ground black pepper

thyme sprigs, to garnish

1 Put the dried porcini in a bowl, add 1 cup warm water and let soak for 20–30 minutes. Lift out of the liquid and squeeze over the bowl to remove as much of the soaking liquid as possible. Strain all the liquid and reserve to use later. Finely chop the porcini.

2 Heat the oil and butter in a large saucepan until foaming. Add the sliced leeks, chopped shallots and garlic and cook gently for about 5 minutes, stirring frequently, until soft.

3 Chop or slice the fresh wild mushrooms and add to the pan. Stir over medium heat for a few minutes, until they begin to soften. Pour in the stock and bring to a boil. Add the porcini, their soaking liquid, the dried thyme and salt and ground black pepper. Lower the heat, half cover the pan and simmer the soup gently for 30 minutes, stirring occasionally.

4 Pour about three-quarters of the soup into a blender or food processor and process until very smooth. Return the purée to the soup remaining in the pan, stir in the cream and heat through. Check the consistency and add a little more stock or water if the soup is too thick. Taste for seasoning. Serve hot garnished with thyme sprigs.

Spinach and Tofu Soup

This soup is really delicious. If fresh spinach is not in season, watercress or lettuce can be used instead.

INGREDIENTS

Serves 4

1 cake tofu, 3-inch sq. and
   1-inch thick
4 ounces spinach leaves
3 cups vegetable stock
1 tablespoon light soy sauce
salt and ground black pepper

1 Rinse the tofu, then cut into 12 small pieces, each about ¼-inch thick. Wash the spinach leaves and cut them into small pieces.

2 In a wok or saucepan, bring the stock to a rolling boil. Add the tofu and soy sauce, bring back to a boil and simmer for about 2 minutes.

3 Add the spinach and simmer for another minute. Skim the surface to make it clear, then add salt and ground black pepper to taste, and serve.

Salmon Chowder

A variation on shrimp chowder, this salmon version is equally delicious.

Serves 4–6

1½ tablespoons butter or margarine

1 onion, minced

1 leek, minced

½ cup minced fennel

¼ cup all-pupose flour

6¼ cups fish stock

8 ounces potatoes, cut into ½-inch cubes
    (about 2 medium-size potatoes)

salt and ground black pepper

1 pound boneless, skinless salmon, cut
    into ¾-inch cubes

¾ cup milk

½ cup whipping cream

2 tablespoons chopped fresh dill

4 Add the cubed salmon and then simmer until just cooked, 3–5 minutes. The cubes should remain intact, not fall apart.

5 Stir in the milk, cream and dill. Cook until just warmed through; do not boil. Taste and adjust the seasoning if necessary, then serve.

1 Melt the butter or margarine in a large saucepan. Add the onion, leek and fennel and cook over medium heat until the vegetables are softened, 5–8 minutes, stirring occasionally.

2 Stir in the flour. Reduce the heat to low and cook, stirring occasionally to prevent any lumps from forming, for 3 minutes.

3 Add the stock and potatoes. Season with salt and ground black pepper. Bring to a boil, then reduce the heat, cover and simmer until the potatoes are tender, about 20 minutes.

Tomato and Blue Cheese Soup with Bacon

As blue cheese is rather salty, it is important to use unsalted stock for this flavorful soup.

Serves 4

3 pounds ripe tomatoes, peeled, quartered and seeded

2 garlic cloves, crushed

2 tablespoons vegetable oil or butter

1 leek, chopped

1 carrot, chopped

4 cups unsalted chicken stock

4 ounces Danish blue cheese, crumbled

3 tablespoons whipping cream

several large fresh basil leaves, or 1–2 fresh parsley sprigs

salt and ground black pepper

6 ounces bacon, cooked and crumbled, to garnish

1 Preheat the oven to 400°F. Spread the tomatoes in a baking dish. Sprinkle with the garlic and some salt and ground black pepper. Bake for 35 minutes.

2 Heat the oil or butter in a large saucepan. Add the leek and carrot and season lightly with salt and pepper. Cook over low heat, stirring often, for 10 minutes or until softened.

3 Stir in the chicken stock and baked tomatoes. Bring to a boil, lower the heat, cover and simmer for 20 minutes.

4 Add the blue cheese, cream, and basil or parsley. Transfer to a food processor or blender and process until smooth (working in batches if necessary). Taste for seasoning; adjust if needed.

5 If necessary, reheat the soup, but do not let it boil. Ladle into warmed bowls and sprinkle on the crumbled bacon.

Tortellini Chanterelle Broth

The savory-sweet quality of chanterelle mushrooms combines well in a simple broth with spinach-and-ricotta-filled tortellini. The addition of a little sherry creates a warming effect.

Serves 4

12 ounces fresh spinach and ricotta
   tortellini, or 6 ounces dried

5 cups chicken stock

5 tablespoons dry sherry

6 ounces fresh chanterelle mushrooms,
   trimmed and sliced, or ½ cup dried
   chanterelles

chopped fresh parsley, to garnish

1 Cook the tortellini according to the package instructions. Bring the chicken stock to a boil, add the dry sherry and fresh or dried mushrooms and simmer for 10 minutes.

2 Strain the tortellini, add to the stock, then ladle the broth into four warmed soup bowls, making sure each contains the same proportions of tortellini and mushrooms. Garnish with the chopped parsley and serve.

French Onion and Morel Soup

French onion soup is appreciated for its light beefy taste. There are few improvements to be made to this classic soup, but a few richly scented morel mushrooms will impart a worthwhile flavor.

Serves 4

4 tablespoons unsalted butter, plus extra
    for spreading

1 tablespoon vegetable oil

3 onions, sliced

3¾ cups beef stock

5 tablespoons Madeira or sherry

8 dried morel mushrooms

4 slices French bread

3 ounces Gruyère, Beaufort or Fontina
    cheese, grated

2 tablespoons chopped fresh parsley

1 Melt the butter with the oil in a large frying pan, then add the sliced onions and cook gently for 10–15 minutes, until the onions are a rich mahogany brown color.

2 Transfer the browned onions to a large saucepan, cover with beef stock, add the Madeira or sherry and the dried morels, then simmer for 20 minutes.

3 Preheat the broiler to medium temperature and toast the French bread on both sides. Spread one side with butter and heap on the grated cheese. Ladle the soup into four flameproof bowls, float the cheesy toasts on top and broil until they are crisp and brown. Alternatively, broil the cheese-topped toast, then place one slice in each warmed soup bowl before ladling on the hot soup. The toast will float to the surface. Sprinkle on the chopped fresh parsley and serve.

COOK'S TIP

The flavor and richness of this soup will improve with keeping. Chill for up to 5 days.

Curried Parsnip Soup

The spices impart a delicious, mild curry flavor which carries an exotic breath of India.

INGREDIENTS

Serves 4

2 tablespoons butter

1 garlic clove, crushed

1 onion, chopped

1 teaspoon ground cumin

1 teaspoon ground coriander

4 parsnips, peeled and sliced

2 teaspoons medium curry paste

scant 2 cups chicken stock

scant 2 cups milk

4 tablespoons sour cream

squeeze of lemon juice

salt and ground black pepper

fresh chives, to garnish

ready-made garlic and cilantro naan,
    to serve

1 Heat the butter in a large pan and add the garlic and onion. Fry gently for 4–5 minutes, until lightly golden. Stir in the cumin and coriander and cook for another 1–2 minutes.

2 Add the parsnips and stir until well coated with the butter, then stir in the curry paste, followed by the stock. Cover the pan and simmer for 15 minutes, until the parsnips are tender.

3 Ladle the soup into a blender or food processor and then process until smooth.

4 Return the soup to the pan and stir in the milk. Heat gently for 2–3 minutes, then add half the sour cream and all the lemon juice. Season well.

5 Serve in bowls topped with swirls of the remaining sour cream and the chopped fresh chives, accompanied by the naan.

Malayan Shrimp Laksa

This spicy shrimp and noodle soup tastes just as good when made with fresh crab meat or any flaked cooked fish. If you are short on time or can't find all the spicy paste ingredients, buy ready-made laksa paste, which is available at Asian stores.

INGREDIENTS

Serves 3–4

4 ounces rice vermicelli or stir-fry
   rice noodles
1 tablespoon vegetable or peanut oil
2½ cups fish stock
1⅔ cups thin coconut milk
2 tablespoons *nam pla* (Thai fish sauce)
½ lime
16–24 cooked peeled shrimp
salt and cayenne pepper
4 tablespoons fresh cilantro sprigs and
   leaves, chopped, to garnish

For the spicy paste
2 lemongrass stalks, finely chopped
2 fresh red chiles, seeded and chopped
1-inch piece fresh ginger, peeled and sliced
½ teaspoon *blachan* (dried shrimp paste)
2 garlic cloves, chopped
½ teaspoon ground turmeric
2 tablespoons tamarind paste

1 Cook the rice vermicelli or noodles in a large saucepan of boiling salted water according to the instructions on the package. Put in a large sieve or colander, then rinse under cold water and drain. Set aside and keep warm.

2 To make the spicy paste, place all the ingredients in a mortar and pound with a pestle. Or, if you prefer, put the ingredients in a food processor or blender and then process until a smooth paste is formed.

3 Heat the oil in a large saucepan, add the spicy paste and fry, stirring constantly, for a few moments to release all the flavors, but be careful not to let it burn.

4 Add the fish stock and coconut milk and bring to a boil. Stir in the *nam pla*, then simmer for 5 minutes. Season with salt and cayenne to taste, adding a squeeze of lime. Add the shrimp and heat through for a few seconds.

5 Divide the noodles among three or four soup plates. Pour on the soup, making sure that each portion includes an equal number of shrimp. Garnish with cilantro and serve piping hot.

Broccoli Soup with Garlic Toast

This is an Italian recipe, originating from Rome. For the best flavor and color, use the freshest broccoli you can find.

INGREDIENTS

Serves 6

1½ pounds broccoli spears

7½ cups chicken or vegetable stock

salt and ground black pepper

2 tablespoons fresh lemon juice

freshly grated Parmesan cheese
  (optional), to serve

For the garlic toast

6 slices white bread

1 large clove garlic, halved

1 Using a small sharp knife, peel the broccoli stems, starting from the base of the stalks and pulling gently up toward the florets. (The peel comes off very easily.) Chop the broccoli into small chunks.

2 Bring the stock to a boil in a large saucepan. Add the chopped broccoli and simmer for 30 minutes or until soft.

COOK'S TIP

As this is an Italian recipe, choose a really good quality Parmesan cheese, if you are using it. The very best is Italy's own Parmigiano-Reggiano.

3 Purée about half of the soup in a blender or food processor and then mix into the rest of the soup. Season with salt, pepper and lemon juice.

4 Just before serving, reheat the soup to just below the boiling point. Toast the bread, rub with garlic and cut into quarters. Place 3 or 4 pieces of toast in the bottom of each soup plate. Ladle on the soup. Serve immediately, with grated Parmesan cheese, if desired.

Spinach and Rice Soup

Use very fresh, young spinach leaves in the preparation of this light and fresh-tasting soup.

INGREDIENTS

Serves 4

1½ pounds fresh spinach, washed

3 tablespoons extra virgin olive oil

1 small onion, finely chopped

2 garlic cloves, finely chopped

1 small fresh red chile, seeded and
　finely chopped

generous 1 cup risotto rice

5 cups vegetable stock

salt and ground black pepper

4 tablespoons grated Pecorino cheese

1 Place the spinach in a large pan with just the water that clings to its leaves after washing. Add a large pinch of salt. Heat gently until the spinach has wilted, then remove from heat and drain, reserving any liquid.

2 Either chop the spinach finely using a large knife or place in a food processor and process to a fairly coarse purée.

> ### COOK'S TIP
>
> Pecorino, made from sheep's milk, has a slightly sharper taste than its cow's milk counterpart, Parmesan. However, if you cannot find it, use Parmesan instead.

3 Heat the oil in a large saucepan and gently cook the onion, garlic and chile for 4–5 minutes, until softened. Stir in the rice until well coated, then pour in the stock and reserved spinach liquid. Bring to a boil, lower the heat and simmer for 10 minutes. Add the spinach, with salt and ground black pepper to taste. Cook for another 5–7 minutes, until the rice is tender. Check the seasoning and adjust if needed. Serve with the Pecorino cheese.

Split Pea Soup

This tasty winter soup is a perfect family appetizer, and can be made using leftover cold ham if necessary.

INGREDIENTS

Serves 4–6

2 tablespoons butter

1 large onion, chopped

1 large celery stalk with leaves, chopped

2 carrots, chopped

1 pound ham bone

8½ cups water

1½ cups split peas

2 tablespoons chopped fresh parsley, plus extra to garnish

½ teaspoon dried thyme

1 bay leaf

about 2 tablespoons lemon juice

salt and ground black pepper

3 After 2 hours, once the peas are very tender, remove the ham bone. Let it cool a bit, then remove the skin and cut the meat from the bones. Discard the skin and bones, then cut the meat into chunks as evenly sized as possible.

4 Return the chunks of ham to the soup. Discard the bay leaf. Taste and adjust the seasoning with more lemon juice, salt and pepper.

5 Serve hot, sprinkled with fresh parsley.

1 Melt the butter in a large heavy saucepan. Add the onion, celery and carrots and cook until soft, stirring occasionally.

2 Place all the rest of the ingredients in the pan. Bring to a boil, cover and simmer gently for 2 hours.

Fish Soup with Rouille

Making this soup is simplicity itself, yet the flavor suggests it is the product of painstaking preparation and complicated cooking.

INGREDIENTS

Serves 6

2¼ pounds mixed fish

2 tablespoons olive oil

1 onion, chopped

1 carrot, chopped

1 leek, chopped

2 large ripe tomatoes, chopped

1 red bell pepper, seeded and chopped

2 garlic cloves, peeled

⅔ cup tomato paste

1 large fresh bouquet garni, containing
    3 parsley sprigs, 3 small celery stalks
    and 3 bay leaves

1¼ cups dry white wine

salt and ground black pepper

For the rouille

2 garlic cloves, roughly chopped

1 teaspoon coarse salt

1 thick slice of white bread, crust
    removed, soaked in water and then
    squeezed dry

1 fresh red chile, seeded and roughly
    chopped

3 tablespoons olive oil

salt, to taste

pinch of cayenne pepper (optional)

For the garnish

12 slices of baguette, toasted

2 ounces Gruyère cheese, finely grated

COOK'S TIP
~
Any firm fish can be used for this recipe. If you use whole fish, include the heads, which enhance the flavor of the soup.

1 Cut the fish into 3-inch chunks, removing any obvious bones. Heat the olive oil in a large saucepan, then add the prepared fish and chopped vegetables. Stir gently until the vegetables begin to color.

2 Add all the other soup ingredients, then pour in just enough cold water to cover the mixture. Season well and bring to just below the boiling point, then lower the heat so that the soup is barely simmering, cover and cook for 1 hour.

3 Meanwhile, make the rouille. Put the garlic and coarse salt in a mortar and crush to a paste with a pestle. Add the soaked bread and chile and pound until smooth, or purée in a food processor. Whisk in the olive oil, a drop at a time, to make a smooth, shiny sauce that resembles mayonnaise. Season with salt and add a pinch of cayenne, if desired. Set aside.

4 Lift out and discard the bouquet garni. Purée the soup in batches in a food processor, then strain through a fine sieve into a clean pan, pushing the solids through with a ladle.

5 Reheat the soup but do not boil. Check the seasoning and ladle into individual bowls. Top each with two slices of toasted baguette, a spoonful of rouille and some grated Gruyére.

PÂTÉS AND TERRINES

Smoked Salmon Pâté

Making this pâté in individual ramekins wrapped in extra smoked salmon gives a really special presentation. Taste the mousse as you are making it, as some people prefer more lemon juice and salt and pepper.

INGREDIENTS

Serves 4

12 ounces thinly sliced smoked salmon (wild if possible)

⅔ cup heavy cream

finely grated zest and juice of 1 lemon

salt and ground black pepper

melba toast, to serve

1 Line four small ramekins with plastic wrap. Then line the dishes with 4 ounces of the smoked salmon cut into strips long enough to flop over the edges.

2 In a food processor fitted with a metal blade, process the rest of the salmon with the cream, lemon zest and juice, salt and plenty of pepper.

3 Pack the lined ramekins with the smoked salmon pâté and wrap over the loose strips of salmon. Cover with plastic wrap and chill for 30 minutes. Invert onto plates; serve with melba toast.

Smoked Haddock Pâté

Arbroath smokies are small haddock that are beheaded and gutted but not split before being salted and hot-smoked, creating a great flavor.

INGREDIENTS

Serves 6

3 large Arbroath smokies, about
   8 ounces each
1¼ cups cream cheese
3 eggs, beaten
2–3 tablespoons lemon juice
ground black pepper
chervil sprigs, to garnish
lemon wedges and lettuce leaves, to serve

1 Preheat the oven to 325°F. Butter six ramekins.

2 Lay the smokies in a baking dish and heat through in the oven for 10 minutes. Carefully remove the skin and bones from the smokies, then flake the flesh into a bowl.

3 Mash the fish with a fork and work in the cheese, then the eggs. Add lemon juice and pepper.

4 Divide the fish mixture among the ramekins and place in a roasting pan. Pour hot water into the roasting pan to come halfway up the dishes. Bake for 30 minutes, until just set.

5 Let cool for 2–3 minutes, then run a knife point around the edge of each dish and invert onto a warmed plate. Garnish with chervil sprigs and serve with the lemon wedges and lettuce.

Chicken Liver Pâté

This rich-tasting, smooth pâté will keep in the refrigerator for about 3 days. Serve with thick slices of hot toast or warmed bread—a rustic olive oil bread such as ciabatta would be a good partner.

INGREDIENTS

Serves 8

4 ounces chicken livers, thawed if frozen,
  trimmed
1 small garlic clove, chopped
1 tablespoon sherry
2 tablespoons brandy
¼ cup butter, melted
¼ teaspoon salt
fresh herbs and black peppercorns,
  to garnish
hot toast or warmed bread, to serve

1 Preheat the oven to 300°F. Place the chicken livers and chopped garlic in a food processor or blender and process until they are smooth.

2 With the motor running, gradually add the sherry, brandy, melted butter and salt.

3 Pour the liver mixture into two 3-inch ramekins. Cover the tops with aluminum foil but do not let the foil come down the sides too far.

4 Place the ramekins in a small roasting pan and pour in boiling water so that it comes about halfway up the sides of the ramekins.

5 Carefully transfer the pan to the oven and bake the pâté for 20 minutes. Let to cool to room temperature, then remove the ramekins from the pan and chill until needed. Serve the pâté with toast or bread, garnished with herbs and peppercorns.

Herbed Liver Pâté Pie

Serve this highly flavored pâté with a glass of Pilsner beer for a change from wine.

Serves 10

1½ pounds ground pork

12 ounces pork liver

2 cups diced cooked ham

1 small onion, finely chopped

2 tablespoons chopped fresh parsley

1 teaspoon German mustard

2 tablespoons Kirsch

1 teaspoon salt

beaten egg, for sealing and glazing

1-ounce envelope aspic jelly

1 cup boiling water

ground black pepper

mustard, bread and dill pickles, to serve

For the pastry

4 cups all-purpose flour

pinch of salt

1¼ cups butter

2 eggs plus 1 egg yolk

2 tablespoons water

1 Preheat the oven to 400°F. To make the pastry, sift the flour and salt and rub in the butter. Beat the eggs, egg yolk and water, add to the dry ingredients and mix.

2 Knead the dough briefly until smooth. Roll out two-thirds on a lightly floured surface and use to line a 4 x 10-inch hinged loaf pan. Trim any excess dough.

3 Process half the pork and all of the liver until fairly smooth. Stir in the remaining ground pork, ham, onion, parsley, mustard, Kirsch, salt and black pepper to taste.

4 Spoon the filling into the pan, smoothing it down and then leveling the surface.

5 Roll out the remaining pastry on the lightly floured surface and use it to top the pie, sealing the edges with some of the beaten egg. Decorate with the pastry trimmings and glaze with the remaining beaten egg. Using a fork, make 3 or 4 holes in the top for the steam to escape.

6 Bake for 40 minutes, then reduce the oven temperature to 350°F and cook for a another hour. Cover the pastry with aluminum foil if the top begins to brown too much. Let the pie cool in the pan.

7 Make the aspic jelly, using the boiling water. Stir to dissolve, then let cool.

8 Make a small hole near the edge of the pie with a skewer, then pour in the aspic through a waxed paper funnel. Chill for at least 2 hours before serving the pie in slices with mustard, bread and dill pickles.

Shrimp, Egg and Avocado Mousse

A light and creamy mousse with lots of chunky texture and a great mix of flavors. Serve on the same day you make it, but chill really well first.

INGREDIENTS

Serves 6

a little olive oil

1 packet gelatin

juice and zest of 1 lemon

4 tablespoons good-quality mayonnaise

4 tablespoons chopped fresh dill

1 teaspoon anchovy extract

1 teaspoon Worcestershire sauce

1 large avocado, ripe but just firm

4 hard-boiled eggs, peeled and chopped

1 cup cooked shrimp (roughly chopped if large)

1 cup heavy or whipping cream, lightly whipped

2 egg whites, whisked

salt and ground black pepper

dill or parsley sprigs, to garnish

warmed whole-grain bread or toast to serve

1 Prepare six small ramekins. Lightly grease the dishes with olive oil, then wrap a waxed paper collar around the top of each and secure with tape. This ensures that you can fill the dishes as high as you like, and the extra mixture will be supported while setting and it will look really dramatic when you remove the paper. Alternatively, prepare just one small soufflé dish.

2 Dissolve the gelatin in the lemon juice with 1 tablespoon hot water in a small bowl set over hot water, until clear, stirring occasionally. Let to cool slightly then blend in the lemon zest, mayonnaise, dill and and anchovy extract and Worcestershire sauce.

3 In a medium bowl mash the avocado; add the eggs and shrimp. Stir in the gelatin mixture and then fold in the cream, egg whites and seasoning to taste. When evenly blended spoon into the ramekins or soufflé dish and chill for 3–4 hours. Garnish with the herbs and serve with bread or toast.

COOK'S TIP

Other fish can be a good alternative to shrimp. Try substituting the same amount of smoked trout or salmon, or cooked crab meat.

Sea Trout Mousse

This deliciously creamy mousse makes a little sea trout go a long way. It is equally good made with salmon if sea trout is unavailable. Serve with crisp melba toast or triangles of lightly toasted pita bread.

INGREDIENTS

Serves 6

9 ounces sea trout fillet

½ cup fish stock

2 gelatin leaves, or 1 tablespoon
     powdered gelatin

juice of ½ lemon

2 tablespoons dry sherry or dry vermouth

2 tablespoons freshly grated Parmesan

1¼ cups whipping cream

2 egg whites

1 tablespoon sunflower oil, for greasing

salt and ground white pepper

For the garnish

2-inch piece cucumber, with peel, thinly
     sliced and halved

fresh dill or chervil

1 Put the sea trout in a shallow pan. Pour in the fish stock and heat to the simmering point. Poach the fish for 3–4 minutes, until it is lightly cooked. Strain the stock into a bowl and let the trout cool slightly.

2 Add the gelatin to the hot stock and stir until it has dissolved completely. Set aside until required.

3 When the trout is cool enough to handle, remove the skin and flake the flesh. Pour the stock into a food processor or blender. Process briefly, then gradually add the flaked trout, lemon juice, sherry or vermouth and Parmesan through the feeder tube, continuing to process the mixture until it is smooth. Scrape into a large bowl and let cool completely.

4 Lightly whip the cream in a bowl; fold it into the cold trout mixture. Season to taste, then cover with plastic wrap and chill in the refrigerator until the mousse is just starting to set. It should have the consistency of mayonnaise.

5 In a grease-free bowl, beat the egg whites with a pinch of salt until they are softly peaking. Then using a large metal spoon, stir about one-third of the egg whites into the sea trout mixture to slacken it slightly, then fold in the rest.

6 Lightly grease six ramekins or similar individual serving dishes. Divide the mousse among the prepared dishes and level the surface. Place in the refrigerator for 2–3 hours, until set. Just before serving, arrange a few slices of cucumber and a small herb sprig on top of each mousse and sprinkle on a little chopped dill or chervil too.

Salmon Rillettes

This is an economical way of serving salmon, with only a little fillet needed per head.

INGREDIENTS

Serves 6

12 ounces salmon fillets

¾ cup butter, softened

1 celery stalk, finely chopped

1 leek, white part only, finely chopped

1 bay leaf

⅔ cup dry white wine

4 ounces smoked salmon trimmings

generous pinch of ground mace

4 tablespoons fromage frais

salt and ground black pepper

salad leaves, to serve

1 Lightly season the salmon. Melt 2 tablespoons of the butter in a medium sauté pan. Add the celery and leek and cook for about 5 minutes. Add the salmon and bay leaf and pour on the white wine. Cover and cook for about 15 minutes, until tender.

2 Strain the cooking liquid into a pan and boil until reduced to 2 tablespoons. Cool. Meanwhile, melt 4 tablespoons of the remaining butter and gently cook the smoked salmon trimmings until it turns pale pink. Let cool.

3 Remove the skin and any bones from the salmon fillets. Flake the flesh into a bowl and add the reduced, cooled cooking liquid.

4 Beat in the remaining butter, with the ground mace and the fromage frais. Break up the cooked smoked salmon trimmings and fold into the salmon mixture with all the juices from the pan. Taste and adjust the seasoning if you need to.

5 Spoon the salmon mixture into a dish or terrine and smooth the top level. Cover with plastic wrap and chill. The prepared mixture can be left in the refrigerator for up to 2 days.

6 To serve the salmon rillettes, shape the mixture into oval quenelles using two teaspoons and arrange on individual plates with the salad leaves. Accompany the rillettes with brown bread, if desired.

Brandade of Salt Cod

There are almost as many versions of this creamy salt cod purée as there are regions of France. Some contain mashed potatoes, others truffles. This comparatively light recipe includes garlic, but you can omit it and serve the brandade on toasted slices of French bread rubbed with garlic, if you prefer.

INGREDIENTS

Serves 6

7 ounces salt cod

1 cup extra virgin olive oil

4 garlic cloves, crushed

1 cup whipping or heavy cream

ground white pepper

shredded scallions, to garnish

herbed crispbread, to serve

1 Soak the fish in cold water for 24 hours, changing the water often. Drain. Cut into pieces, place in a shallow pan and pour in cold water to cover. Heat the water until simmering, then poach the fish for 8 minutes, until it is just cooked. Drain, then remove the skin and bone the cod carefully.

2 Combine the olive oil and garlic in a small saucepan and heat to just below the boiling point. In another saucepan, heat the cream until it starts to simmer.

3 Put the cod into a food processor, process it briefly, then gradually add alternate amounts of the garlic-flavored olive oil and cream, while keeping the machine running.

4 Once the mixture has the consistency of mashed potatoes, add white pepper to taste, then scoop the branade into a serving bowl. Garnish with shredded scallions and serve warm with herbed crispbread.

COOK'S TIP

You can purée the fish mixture in a mortar with a pestle. This gives a better texture but is notoriously hard work.

Potted Salmon with Lemon and Dill

This sophisticated appetizer would be ideal for a dinner party. Preparation is done well in advance, so you can concentrate on the main course or, if you are really well organized, you can enjoy a pre-dinner conversation with your guests. If you cannot find fresh dill, use 1 teaspoon dried dill instead.

INGREDIENTS

Serves 6

12 ounces cooked salmon, skinned

⅔ cup butter, softened

zest and juice of 1 large lemon

2 teaspoons chopped fresh dill

salt and ground white pepper

¾ cup sliced almonds, roughly chopped

1 Flake the salmon into a bowl and then place in a food processor together with two-thirds of the butter, the lemon zest and juice, half the dill, and plenty of salt and pepper. Blend until the mixture is quite smooth.

2 Mix in the sliced almonds. Check the seasoning and pack the mixture into small ramekins.

3 Sprinkle the other half of the dill on top of each ramekin. Clarify the remaining butter, and pour onto each ramekin to make a seal. Chill. Serve with crudités.

Potted Shrimp

The tiny brown shrimp that were traditionally used for potting are very hard to peel. Since they are rare nowadays, it is easier to use peeled cooked medium shrimp instead.

INGREDIENTS

Serves 4

2 cups shelled shrimp

1 cup butter

pinch of ground mace

salt, to taste

cayenne pepper

dill sprigs, to garnish

lemon wedges and thin slices of brown
   bread and butter, to serve

1 Chop a quarter of the shrimp. Melt ½ cup of the butter slowly, carefully skimming off any foam that rises to the surface with a metal spoon.

2 Stir all the shrimp, the mace, salt and cayenne into the pan and heat gently without boiling. Pour the shrimp and butter mixture into four individual pots and let cool.

3 Heat the remaining butter in a clean small saucepan, then carefully spoon the clear butter onto the shrimp, leaving behind the sediment.

4 Leave until the butter is almost set, then place a dill sprig in the center of each pot. Let set completely, then cover and chill.

5 Transfer the shrimp to room temperature 30 minutes before serving with lemon wedges for squeezing on and thin slices of brown bread and butter.

COOK'S TIP

If you prefer add a pinch of freshly grated nutmeg in place of the ground mace. The flavor is similar, but it will not color the dish.

Broiled Vegetable Terrine

A colorful, layered terrine, this appetizer uses all the vegetables that are associated with the Mediterranean and long, balmy summer evenings.

Serves 6

2 large red bell peppers, quartered, cored and seeded

2 large yellow bell peppers, quartered, cored and seeded

1 large eggplant, sliced lengthwise

2 large zucchini, sliced lengthwise

6 tablespoons olive oil

1 large red onion, thinly sliced

½ cup raisins

1 tablespoon tomato paste

1 tablespoon red wine vinegar

1⅔ cups tomato juice

2 tablespoons powdered gelatin

fresh basil leaves, to garnish

For the dressing

6 tablespoons extra virgin olive oil

2 tablespoons red wine vinegar

salt and ground black pepper

1 Place the prepared peppers skin side up under a hot broiler and cook until the skins are blackened. Transfer to a bowl and cover with a plate. Let cool.

2 Arrange the eggplant and zucchini slices on separate baking sheets. Brush them with a little oil and cook under the broiler, turning occasionally, until they are tender and golden.

3 Heat the remaining olive oil in a frying pan, and add the sliced onion, raisins, tomato purée and red wine vinegar. Cook gently until the mixture is soft and syrupy. Set aside and let cool in the frying pan.

4 Line a 7½-cup terrine with plastic wrap, (it helps if you lightly oil the terrine first) leaving a little hanging over the sides of the container.

5 Pour half the tomato juice into a saucepan, and sprinkle with the gelatin. Dissolve gently over low heat, stirring to prevent any lumps from forming.

6 Place a layer of red peppers in the bottom of the terrine, and pour in enough of the tomato juice with gelatin to cover.

7 Continue layering the vegetables, pouring tomato juice over each layer. Finishing with a layer of red peppers. Add the remaining tomato juice to the pan, and pour into the terrine. Give it a sharp tap, to disperse the juice. Cover and chill until set.

8 To make the dressing, whisk together the oil and vinegar, and season. Turn out the terrine and remove the plastic wrap. Serve in thick slices, drizzled with dressing and garnished with basil leaves.

COOK'S TIP

For a change, use yellow and orange bell peppers along with or instead of the red and green ones. Green beans, simply boiled first, would make a nice addition, as would a layer of peas or corn.

Roast Bell Pepper Terrine

This terrine is perfect for a dinner party because it tastes better if made ahead. Prepare the salsa on the day of serving. Serve with a warmed Italian bread such as ciabatta or the flavorful focaccia.

INGREDIENTS

Serves 8

8 bell peppers (red, yellow and orange)

3 cups mascarpone cheese

3 eggs, separated

2 tablespoons each roughly chopped
    flat-leaf parsley and shredded basil

2 large garlic cloves, roughly chopped

2 red, yellow or orange bell peppers,
    seeded and roughly chopped

2 tablespoons extra virgin olive oil

2 teaspoons balsamic vinegar

a few basil sprigs

salt and ground black pepper

1 Place the whole peppers under a hot broiler for 8–10 minutes, turning frequently. Then put into a plastic bag until cold before skinning and seeding them. Chop seven of the peppers lengthwise into thin strips.

2 Put the mascarpone cheese in a bowl with the egg yolks, herbs and half the garlic. Add salt and pepper to taste. Beat well. In a separate bowl, whisk the egg whites into soft peaks, then fold into the cheese mixture until they are evenly incorporated.

3 Preheat the oven to 350°F. Line the bottom of a lightly oiled 2-pound loaf pan. Put one-third of the cheese mixture in the pan and spread level. Arrange half the pepper strips on top in an even layer. Repeat until all the cheese and peppers are used, ending with a layer of the cheese mixture.

4 Cover the pan with aluminum foil and place in a roasting pan. Pour in boiling water to come halfway up the sides of the pan. Bake for 1 hour. Let cool in the water bath, then lift out and chill overnight.

5 A few hours before serving, make the salsa. Place the remaining skinned pepper and fresh peppers in a food processor. Add the remaining garlic, oil and vinegar. Set aside a few basil leaves for garnishing and add the rest to the processor. Process until finely chopped. Put the mixture in a bowl, add salt and pepper to taste and mix well. Cover and chill until ready to serve.

6 Turn out the terrine, peel off the lining paper and slice thickly. Garnish with the reserved basil leaves and serve cold, with the sweet pepper salsa.

Asparagus and Egg Terrine

For a special dinner this terrine is a delicious choice, yet it is very light. Make the hollandaise sauce well in advance and warm through gently when needed.

INGREDIENTS

Serves 8

²⁄₃ cup milk

²⁄₃ cup heavy cream

3 tablespoons butter

3 tablespoons all-purpose flour

3 ounces herbed or garlic cream cheese

1½ pounds asparagus spears, cooked

a little oil

2 eggs, separated

1 tablespoon snipped fresh chives

2 tablespoons chopped fresh dill

salt and ground black pepper

dill sprigs, to garnish

For the orange hollandaise sauce

1 tablespoon white wine vinegar

1 tablespoon fresh orange juice

4 black peppercorns

1 bay leaf

2 egg yolks

½ cup butter, melted and cooled slightly

1 Put the milk and cream into a small saucepan and heat to just below the boiling point. Melt the butter in a medium pan, stir in the flour and cook into a thick paste. Gradually stir in the milk, whisking as it thickens and beat to a smooth paste. Stir in the cream cheese, season to taste with salt and ground black pepper and let cool slightly.

2 Trim the asparagus to fit the width of a 5-cup bread pan or terrine. Lightly oil the pan and then place a sheet of waxed paper in the bottom, cut to fit. Preheat the oven to 350°F.

3 Beat the yolks into the sauce mixture. Whisk the whites until stiff and fold in with the chives, dill and seasoning. Layer the asparagus and egg mixture in the pan, starting and finishing with asparagus. Cover the top with aluminum foil.

4 Place the terrine in a roasting pan; half fill with hot water. Cook for 45–55 minutes, until firm.

5 To make the sauce, put the vinegar, juice, peppercorns and bay leaf in a small pan and heat until reduced by half.

6 Cool the sauce slightly, then whisk in the egg yolks, then the butter, with a balloon whisk over very low heat. Season to taste and keep whisking until thick. Keep the sauce warm over a pan of hot water.

7 When the terrine is just firm to the touch remove from the oven and let cool, then chill. Carefully invert it onto a serving dish, remove the waxed paper and garnish with the dill. Cut into slices and pour on the warmed sauce.

Haddock and Smoked Salmon Terrine

This is a fairly substantial terrine, so serve modest slices, perhaps accompanied by fresh dill mayonnaise or a fresh mango salsa. Follow with a light main course and a fruit-based dessert.

INGREDIENTS

Serves 10–12

1 tablespoon sunflower oil,
    for greasing
12 ounces oak-smoked salmon
2 pounds haddock fillets, skinned
2 eggs, lightly beaten
7 tablespoons crème fraîche
2 tablespoons drained capers
2 tablespoons drained soft green or
    pink peppercorns
salt and ground white pepper
crème fraîche, peppercorns and fresh dill
    and arugula leaves, to garnish

1 Preheat the oven to 400°F. Grease a 4-cup loaf pan or terrine with the sunflower oil. Use some of the smoked salmon to line the loaf pan or terrine, letting some of the ends overhang the mold. Reserve the remaining smoked salmon until needed.

2 Cut two long slices of haddock the length of the pan or terrine and set aside. Cut the rest of the haddock into small pieces. Season all of the haddock with salt and ground white pepper.

3 Combine the eggs, crème fraîche, capers and green or pink peppercorns in a bowl. Add salt and pepper; stir in the haddock pieces. Spoon the mixture into the mold until it is one-third full. Smooth the surface with a spatula.

4 Wrap the long haddock fillets in the reserved salmon. Lay them on top of the layer of the fish mixture in the pan or terrine.

5 Cover with the rest of the fish mixture, smooth the surface and fold the overhanging pieces of salmon over the top. Cover tightly with a double thickness of aluminum foil. Tap the terrine to settle the contents.

6 Stand the terrine in a roasting pan and pour in boiling water to come halfway up the sides. Place in the oven and cook for 45 minutes—1 hour, until the filling is just set.

7 Take the terrine out of the roasting pan, but do not remove the aluminum foil cover. Place large heavy cans on the foil to weight it and leave until cold. Chill in the refrigerator for 24 hours.

8 About an hour before serving, remove the terrine from the refrigerator, remove the weights and the aluminum foil. Carefully invert onto a serving plate and garnish with crème fraîche, peppercorns, sprigs of dill and arugula leaves.

COOK'S TIP

Use any thick white fish fillets for this terrine; try cod, whiting, hake or hoki.

Striped Fish Terrine

Serve this terrine cold or just warm, with a hollandaise sauce, if desired.

INGREDIENTS

Serves 8

1 tablespoon sunflower oil

1 pound salmon fillet, skinned

1 pound sole fillets, skinned

3 egg whites

7 tablespoons heavy cream

1 tablespoon finely snipped fresh chives

juice of 1 lemon

scant 1 cup fresh or frozen
    peas, cooked

1 teaspoon chopped fresh mint

salt, ground white pepper and
    grated nutmeg

thinly sliced cucumber, watercress and
    whole chives, to garnish

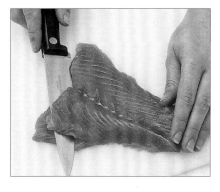

1 Grease a 4-cup loaf pan or terrine with the oil. Slice the salmon thinly; cut it and the sole into long strips, 1 inch wide. Preheat the oven to 400°F.

2 Line the terrine neatly with alternating slices of salmon and sole, leaving the ends overhanging the edge. You should be left with about a third of the salmon and half the sole.

3 In a grease-free bowl, beat the egg whites with a pinch of salt until they form soft peaks. Purée the remaining sole in a food processor. Spoon into a mixing bowl, season, then fold in two-thirds of the egg whites, followed by two-thirds of the cream. Put half the mixture into a second bowl; stir in the chives. Add nutmeg to the first bowl.

4 Purée the remaining salmon, scrape it into a bowl; add the lemon juice. Fold in the remaining egg whites, then the remaining cream.

5 Purée the peas with the mint. Season the mixture and spread it on the bottom of the terrine, smoothing the surface with a spatula. Spoon over the sole with chives mixture and spread evenly.

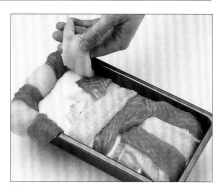

6 Add the salmon mixture, then finish with the plain sole mixture. Cover with the overhanging fish fillets and make a lid of buttered aluminum foil. Stand the terrine in a roasting pan and pour in enough boiling water to come halfway up the sides.

7 Bake for 15–20 minutes, until the top fillets are just cooked and the mousse feels springy. Remove the aluminum foil, lay a wire rack over the top of the terrine and invert both rack and terrine onto an edged baking sheet to catch the cooking juices that drain out. Keep these to make fish stock or soup.

8 Leaving the pan in place, let the terrine stand for about 15 minutes, then turn it over again, invert it onto a serving dish and lift off the pan carefully. Serve warm, or chill in the refrigerator first and serve cold. Garnish with thinly sliced cucumber, watercress and chives before serving.

Turkey, Juniper and Peppercorn Terrine

This is an ideal dish for entertaining, as it can be made several days in advance. If you prefer, arrange some of the pancetta and pistachios as a layer in the middle of the terrine.

INGREDIENTS

Serves 10–12

8 ounces chicken livers, trimmed

1 pound ground turkey

1 pound ground pork

8 ounces cubetti pancetta

½ cup shelled pistachios, roughly chopped

1 teaspoon salt

½ teaspoon ground mace

2 garlic cloves, crushed

1 teaspoon drained green peppercorns
   in brine

1 teaspoon juniper berries

½ cup dry white wine

2 tablespoons gin

finely grated zest of 1 orange

8 large vacuum-packed grape leaves
   in brine

oil, for greasing

1 Chop the chicken livers finely. Put them in a bowl and add the turkey, pork, pancetta, pistachios, salt, mace and garlic. Mix well.

2 Lightly crush the peppercorns and juniper berries and add them to the mixture. Stir in the white wine, gin and orange zest. Cover and chill overnight to let the flavors mingle.

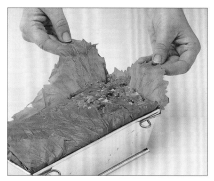

3 Preheat the oven to 325°F. Rinse the grape leaves under cold running water. Drain them thoroughly. Lightly oil a 5-cup pâté terrine or loaf pan. Line the terrine or pan with the leaves, letting the ends hang over the sides. Pack the mixture into the terrine or pan and fold the leaves over to enclose the filling. Brush lightly with oil.

4 Cover the terrine with its lid or with aluminum foil. Place it in a roasting pan and pour in boiling water to come halfway up the sides of the terrine. Bake for 1¾ hours, checking the level of the water occasionally, so that the roasting pan does not dry out.

5 Let the terrine cool, then pour off the surface juices. Cover with plastic wrap, then aluminum foil and place weights on top. Chill in the refrigerator overnight. Serve at room temperature with pickles or chutney, such as spiced kumquats or red bell pepper and chili jelly.

Chicken and Pork Terrine

This pale, elegant terrine is flecked with green peppercorns and parsley, which give it a wonderfully subtle flavor.

INGREDIENTS

Serves 6–8

8 ounces bacon

13 ounces boneless chicken breast, skinned

1 tablespoon lemon juice

8 ounces lean ground pork

½ small onion, finely chopped

2 eggs, beaten

2 tablespoons chopped fresh parsley

1 teaspoon salt

1 teaspoon green peppercorns, crushed

oil, for greasing

salad greens, radishes and lemon wedges, to serve

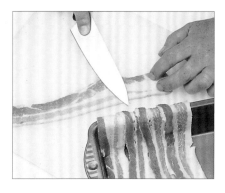

1 Preheat the oven to 325°F. Put the bacon on a board and stretch it using the back of a knife before arranging it in overlapping slices on the bottom and sides of a 2-pound loaf pan.

2 Cut 4 ounces of the chicken into strips about 4 inches long. Sprinkle with lemon juice. Put the rest of the chicken in a food processor or blender with the ground pork and the onion. Process until fairly smooth.

3 Add the eggs, parsley, salt and peppercorns to the meat mixture and process again briefly. Spoon half the mixture into the loaf pan and then level the surface.

4 Arrange the chicken strips on top, then spoon in the remaining meat mixture and smooth the top. Give the pan a couple of sharp taps to knock out any pockets of air.

5 Cover the loaf pan with a piece of oiled aluminum foil and put it in a roasting pan. Pour in enough hot water to come halfway up the sides of the loaf pan. Bake for 45–50 minutes, until firm.

6 Let the terrine cool in the pan before turning out and chilling. Serve sliced, with salad greens, radishes and wedges of lemon for squeezing.

COOK'S TIP

For a slightly sharper flavor, substitute chopped fresh cilantro for the parsley. It goes well with the lemon.

VEGETARIAN

Potato Skewers with Mustard Dip

Potatoes cooked on the grill have a great flavor and crisp skin. Try these delicious kebabs served with a thick, garlic-rich dip for an unusual start to a meal.

INGREDIENTS

Serves 6

For the dip

4 garlic cloves, crushed

2 egg yolks

2 tablespoons lemon juice

1¼ cups extra virgin olive oil

2 teaspoons whole-grain mustard

salt and ground black pepper

For the skewers

2¼ pounds small new potatoes

7 ounces shallots, halved

2 tablespoons olive oil

1 tablespoon sea salt

1 Prepare the grill or preheat the broiler. To make the dip, place the garlic, egg yolks and lemon juice in a blender or a food processor fitted with a metal blade and process for just a few seconds until the mixture is smooth.

2 Keep the blender motor running and add the oil very gradually, pouring it in a thin stream, until the mixture forms a thick, glossy cream. Add the mustard and stir the ingredients together, then season with salt and pepper. Chill until ready to use.

3 Parboil the potatoes in their skins in boiling water for 5 minutes. Drain well and then thread them onto metal skewers, alternating with the shallots.

4 Brush the skewers with oil and sprinkle with salt. Grill or broil for 10–12 minutes, turning occasionally. Serve with the mustard dip.

COOK'S TIP

Only early or "new" potatoes and salad potatoes have the firmness necessary to stay on the skewers.

Grilled Tomatoes on Soda Bread

Nothing could be simpler than this delightful appetizer, yet a drizzle of olive oil and balsamic vinegar and shavings of Parmesan cheese transform it into something really rather special.

Serves 4

olive oil, for brushing and drizzling

6 tomatoes, thickly sliced

4 thick slices soda bread

balsamic vinegar, for drizzling

salt and ground black pepper

shavings of Parmesan cheese, to serve

1 Brush a grill pan with olive oil and heat. Add the tomato slices and cook them for about 4 minutes, turning once, until softened and slightly blackened. Alternatively, heat the broiler to high and line the rack with aluminum foil. Broil the tomato slices for 4–6 minutes, turning once, until softened.

2 Meanwhile, lightly toast the soda bread. Place the tomatoes on top of the toast and drizzle each portion with a little olive oil and balsamic vinegar. Season to taste and serve immediately with thin shavings of Parmesan cheese.

COOK'S TIP

Using a grill pan reduces the amount of oil needed for cooking the tomatoes which is useful for those watching their weight. It also gives them a delicious smoky flavor.

Marinated Feta Cheese with Capers

Marinating cubes of feta cheese with herbs and spices gives a great flavor. Serve with toast.

INGREDIENTS

Serves 6

12 ounces feta cheese
2 garlic cloves
½ teaspoon mixed peppercorns
8 coriander seeds
1 bay leaf
1–2 tablespoons drained capers
oregano or thyme sprigs
olive oil, to cover
hot toast, to serve

1 Cut the feta cheese into cubes. Thickly slice the garlic. Put the mixed peppercorns and coriander seeds in a mortar and crush lightly with a pestle.

2 Pack the feta cubes into a large preserving jar with the bay leaf, interspersing layers of cheese with garlic, crushed peppercorns and coriander, capers and the fresh oregano or thyme sprigs.

3 Pour in enough olive oil to cover the cheese. Close tightly and let marinate for two weeks in the refrigerator.

4 Lift out the feta cubes and serve on hot toast, with some chopped tomatoes and a little of the flavored oil from the jar drizzled on top.

COOK'S TIP

Add pitted black or green olives to the feta cheese in the marinade, if desired.

Cannellini Bean and Rosemary Bruschetta

This delicious Italian recipe makes an unusual but sophisticated appetizer.

INGREDIENTS

Serves 6

⅔ cup dried cannellini beans

5 tomatoes

3 tablespoons olive oil, plus extra
  for drizzling

2 sun-dried tomatoes in oil, drained and
  finely chopped

1 garlic clove, crushed

2 tablespoons chopped fresh rosemary

12 slices Italian-style bread, such
  as ciabatta

1 large garlic clove

salt and ground black pepper

handful of fresh basil leaves, to garnish

1 Put the beans in a bowl, cover in water and soak overnight. Drain and rinse the beans, then place in a saucepan and cover with fresh water. Bring to a boil and boil rapidly for 10 minutes. Then simmer for 50–60 minutes or until tender. Drain, return to the pan and keep warm.

2 Meanwhile, place the tomatoes in a bowl, cover with boiling water; leave for 30 seconds, then peel, seed and chop the flesh. Heat the oil in a frying pan, add the fresh and sun-dried tomatoes, garlic and rosemary. Cook for 2 minutes, until the tomatoes begin to break down and soften.

3 Add the tomato mixture to the cannellini beans and season to taste. Combine well. Keep the bean mixture warm.

4 Rub the cut sides of the bread slices with the garlic clove, then toast them lightly. Spoon the cannellini bean mixture on top of the toast. Sprinkle with basil leaves and drizzle on a little extra olive oil before serving.

Greek Eggplant and Spinach Pie

Eggplant layered with spinach, feta cheese and rice make a flavorful and dramatic filling for a pie. It can be served warm or cold in elegant slices.

Serves 12

13 ounces shortcrust pastry, thawed
   if frozen

3–4 tablespoons olive oil

1 large eggplant, sliced into rounds

1 onion, chopped

1 garlic clove, crushed

6 ounces spinach, washed

4 eggs

½ cup crumbled feta cheese

½ cup freshly grated Parmesan cheese

4 tablespoons plain yogurt

6 tablespoons whole milk

2 cups cooked white or brown long
   grain rice

salt and ground black pepper

2 Heat 2–3 tablespoons of the oil in a frying pan and fry the eggplant slices for 6–8 minutes on each side until golden. You may need to add a little more oil at first, but this will be released as the flesh softens. Lift out and drain well on paper towels.

3 Add the onion and garlic to the oil remaining in the pan then fry over low heat for 4–5 minutes, until soft, adding a little extra oil if necessary.

1 Preheat the oven to 350°F. Roll out the pastry thinly and use to line a 10-inch tart pan. Prick the bottom all over and bake for 10–12 minutes, until the pastry is pale golden. (Alternatively, bake blind, having lined the pastry with baking parchment and weighted it with a handful of baking beans.)

4 Chop the spinach finely, by hand or in a food processor. Beat the eggs in a large mixing bowl, then add the spinach, feta, Parmesan, yogurt, milk and the onion mixture. Season well with salt and ground black pepper and stir thoroughly to mix.

5 Spread the rice in an even layer on the bottom of the part-baked pastry shell. Reserve a few eggplant slices for the top, and arrange the rest in an even layer on the rice.

6 Spoon the spinach and feta mixture onto the eggplant and place the remaining slices on top. Bake for 30–40 minutes, until lightly browned. Serve the pie while warm, or let it cool completely before transferring to a serving plate.

COOK'S TIP

Zucchini could be used in place of the eggplant, if you prefer. Fry the sliced zucchini in a little oil for 3–4 minutes, until they are evenly golden. You will need to use three to four standard zucchini, or choose baby zucchini instead and slice them horizontally.

Glamorgan Sausages

These tasty sausages are ideal for vegetarians, as they are made from cheese and leeks rather than meat.

Makes 8

2½ cups fresh bread crumbs

5 ounces generous cup grated
  Caerphilly cheese

1 small leek, very finely chopped

1 tablespoon chopped fresh parsley

leaves from 1 thyme sprig, chopped

2 eggs

1½ teaspoons English mustard powder

about 3 tablespoons milk

all-purpose flour, for coating

1 tablespoon oil

1 tablespoon butter, melted

salt and ground black pepper

salad leaves and tomato halves, to serve

1 Mix the bread crumbs, cheese, leek, herbs and seasoning. Whisk the eggs with the mustard and reserve 2 tablespoons. Stir the rest into the cheese mixture with enough milk to bind.

2 Divide the cheese mixture into eight portions and form into sausage shapes.

3 Dip the sausages in the reserved egg to coat. Season the flour, then roll the sausages in it to give a light, even coating. Chill for about 30 minutes, until firm.

4 Preheat the broiler and oil a broiler pan. Mix the oil and melted butter and use to brush on the sausages. Broil the sausages for 5–10 minutes, turning them carefully every now and then, until golden brown all over. Serve hot or cold, with salad leaves and tomato halves.

Birds' Nests

A recipe from an old handwritten cookbook from 1887. These are also known as Welsh Eggs because they resemble Scotch Eggs, but they have leeks in the filling.

INGREDIENTS

Serves 6

6 eggs, hard-boiled

flour, seasoned with salt and paprika

1 leek, chopped

2 teaspoons sunflower oil

2 cups fresh white bread crumbs

grated zest and juice of 1 lemon

1/2 cup vegetarian shredded suet

4 tablespoons chopped fresh parsley

1 teaspoon dried thyme

salt and ground black pepper

1 egg, beaten

1/2 cup dried bread crumbs

oil, for deep-frying

lettuce and tomato wedges, to garnish

1 Peel the hard-boiled eggs and toss in the seasoned flour. Set aside until needed.

2 Fry the leeks in the sunflower oil for about 3 minutes, until softened but not browned. Remove from the heat and let cool, then mix with the fresh bread crumbs, lemon zest and juice, suet, herbs and salt and pepper. If the mixture is a bit too dry add a little water.

3 Shape the mixture around the eggs, molding it firmly with your hands, then toss first into the beaten egg and then the dried bread crumbs. Set aside on a plate to chill for 30 minutes. This will firm them up before cooking.

4 Pour enough oil to fill to one-third full a deep-fat fryer and heat to 375°F. Fry the eggs for about 3 minutes in two batches. Remove and drain on paper towels.

5 Serve cool, cut in half to reveal the "birds' nest," garnished with lettuce and tomato wedges.

Son-in-law Eggs

This fascinating name comes from a story about a prospective bridegroom who wanted to impress his future mother-in-law and devised a recipe from the only other dish he knew how to make—boiled eggs. The hard-boiled eggs are deep-fried and then drenched with a sweet piquant tamarind sauce.

INGREDIENTS

Serves 4–6

generous ⅓ cup sugar

4 tablespoons light soy sauce

7 tablespoons tamarind juice

oil, for frying

6 shallots, finely sliced

6 garlic cloves, finely sliced

6 red chiles, sliced

6 hard-boiled eggs, shelled

cilantro sprigs, to garnish

lettuce, to serve

1 Combine the sugar, fish sauce and tamarind juice in a small saucepan. Bring to a boil, stirring until the sugar dissolves, then simmer the sauce for about 5 minutes.

2 Taste and add more sugar, fish sauce or tamarind juice, if necessary. It should be sweet, salty and slightly sour. Transfer the sauce to a bowl and set aside until needed.

3 Heat a couple of spoonfuls of the oil in a frying pan and fry the shallots, garlic and chiles until golden brown. Transfer the mixture to a bowl and set aside.

4 Deep-fry the eggs in hot oil for 3–5 minutes until golden brown. Drain on paper towels, quarter and arrange on a bed of lettuce. Sprinkle on the shallot mixture, drizzle with the sauce and garnish with cilantro.

Dolmades

These stuffed grape leaves originated in Greece. If you can't locate fresh grape leaves, use a package or can of brined leaves. Soak in hot water for 20 minutes, then rinse and dry well on paper towels before use.

INGREDIENTS

Makes 20 to 24

24–28 fresh young grape leaves, soaked

2 tablespoons olive oil

1 large onion, finely chopped

1 garlic clove, crushed

2 cups cooked long grain rice, or mixed white and wild rice

about 3 tablespoons pine nuts

1 tablespoon sliced almonds

¼ cup golden raisins

1 tablespoon snipped fresh chives

1 tablespoon finely chopped fresh mint

juice of ½ lemon

⅔ cup white wine

hot vegetable stock

salt and ground black pepper

mint sprig, to garnish

garlic yogurt and pita bread, to serve

1 Bring a large pan of water to a boil and cook the grape leaves for 2–3 minutes. They will darken and get limp after about 1 minute, and simmering for another minute or so will ensure that they are pliable. If using packaged or canned leaves, place in a bowl, cover with boiling water and leave for 20 minutes, until the leaves can be separated easily. Rinse and dry on paper towels.

2 Heat the oil in a small frying pan and fry the onion and garlic for 3–4 minutes over low heat, until soft. Spoon the mixture into a large bowl and add the cooked rice. Stir to combine.

3 Stir in 2 tablespoons of the pine nuts, the almonds, golden raisins, chives and mint. Squeeze in the lemon juice. Add salt and pepper to taste and mix well.

4 Set aside four large grape leaves. Lay a grape leaf on a clean work surface, veined side facing up. Place a spoonful of filling near the stem and fold the lower part of the grape leaf over it and roll up, folding in the sides as you go. Stuff the rest of the grape leaves in the same way.

5 Line the bottom of a deep frying pan with the reserved grape leaves. Place the dolmades close together in the pan, seam side down, in a single layer. Pour in the wine and enough stock to just cover. Anchor the dolmades by placing a plate on top of them, then cover the pan and simmer gently for 30 minutes.

6 Transfer the dolmades to a plate. Cool, chill, then garnish with the remaining pine nuts and the mint. Serve with a little garlic yogurt and some pita bread.

Poached Eggs Florentine

The term "à la Florentine" means "in the style of Florence" and refers to dishes cooked with spinach and topped with mornay sauce. Here is a subtly spiced, elegant appetizer.

INGREDIENTS

Serves 4

1½ pounds spinach, washed and drained

2 tablespoons butter

4 tablespoons heavy cream

pinch of freshly grated nutmeg

salt and ground black pepper

For the topping

2 tablespoons butter

¼ cup all-purpose flour

1¼ cups hot milk

pinch of ground mace

4 ounces Gruyère cheese, grated

4 eggs

1 tablespoon freshly grated
   Parmesan cheese, plus shavings to serve

1 Place the spinach in a large pan with very little water. Cook for 3–4 minutes or until tender, then drain and chop finely. Return the spinach to the pan, add the butter, cream, nutmeg and seasoning and heat through. Place on the bottom of one large or four small gratin dishes.

2 To make the topping, heat the butter in a small pan, add the flour and cook for 1 minute into a paste. Gradually blend in the hot milk, beating well as it thickens to break up any lumps.

3 Cook for 1–2 minutes, stirring. Remove from the heat and stir in the mace and three-quarters of the Gruyère cheese.

4 Preheat the oven to 400°F. Poach the eggs in lightly salted water for 3–4 minutes. Make hollows in the spinach with the back of a spoon, and place a poached egg in each one. Cover with the cheese sauce and sprinkle on the remaining Gruyère and Parmesan. Bake for 10 minutes or until golden. Serve immediately with Parmesan shavings.

Chili Cheese Tortilla with Tomato Salsa

Good warm or cold, this is like a quiche without the pastry crust. Cheese and chiles are a perfect match for each other.

INGREDIENTS

Serves 8

3 tablespoons sunflower or olive oil

1 small onion, thinly sliced

2–3 green jalapeño chiles, sliced

7 ounces cold cooked potato, thinly sliced

generous 1 cup grated Manchego, Mexican queso blanco or Monterey Jack cheese

6 eggs, beaten

salt and ground black pepper

fresh herbs, to garnish

For the salsa

1¼ pound fresh flavorful tomatoes, peeled, seeded and finely chopped

1 green chile, seeded and finely chopped

2 garlic cloves, crushed

3 tablespoons chopped cilantro

juice of 1 lime

½ teaspoon salt

1 Make the salsa. Put the tomatoes in a bowl with the rest of the ingredients. Mix well and set aside.

COOK'S TIP

If you cannot find the cheeses listed, use a medium Cheddar instead.

2 Heat half the oil in a large omelet pan and gently fry the onion and jalapeños for 5 minutes, stirring once or twice, until softened. Add the potato and cook for another 5 minutes until lightly browned, being careful to keep the slices whole.

3 Using a slotted spoon, transfer the vegetables to a warm plate. Wipe the pan with paper towels, then pour in the remaining oil. Heat well and return the vegetable mixture to the pan. Sprinkle the cheese on top.

4 Pour in the beaten egg, making sure that it seeps under the vegetables. Cook the tortilla over low heat until set. Serve in wedges, garnished with fresh herbs, with the salsa on the side.

Baked Mediterranean Vegetables

Crisp and golden crunchy batter surrounds these vegetables, turning them into a substantial appetizer. Use other vegetables instead, if you prefer.

INGREDIENTS

Serves 10–12

1 small eggplant, trimmed, halved and
    thickly sliced
1 egg
1 cup all-purpose flour
1¼ cups milk
2 tablespoons fresh thyme leaves, or
    2 teaspoons dried
1 red onion
2 large zucchini
1 red bell pepper
1 yellow bell pepper
4–5 tablespoons sunflower oil
salt and ground black pepper
2 tablespoons freshly grated
    Parmesan cheese and fresh herbs,
    to garnish

1 Place the eggplant in a colander or sieve, sprinkle generously with salt and leave for 10 minutes. Drain and pat dry on paper towels.

2 Meanwhile, to make the batter, beat the egg, then gradually beat in the flour and a little milk to make a smooth thick paste. Blend in the rest of the milk, add the thyme leaves and seasoning to taste and blend until smooth. Set in a cool place until needed.

3 Quarter the onion and slice the zucchini and seed and quarter the peppers. Put the oil in a roasting pan and heat through in the oven at 425°F. Add all the vegetables, turn in the fat to coat them well and return to the oven for 20 minutes, until they start to cook.

4 Give the batter another whisk then pour onto the vegetables and return to the oven for 30 minutes. If puffed up and golden, then reduce the heat to 375°F for another 10–15 minutes, until crisp around the edges. Sprinkle with Parmesan and herbs and serve.

COOK'S TIP

It is essential to get the fat in the dish really hot before adding the batter, or it will not rise well. Use a dish which is not too deep.

Zucchini Fritters with Chili Jam

*Chili jam is hot, sweet and sticky—
much like a thick chutney. It adds
a delicious piquancy to these light
zucchini fritters, which are always a
popular dish.*

INGREDIENTS

Makes 12 Fritters

3½ cups coarsely grated zucchini

⅔ cup freshly grated Parmesan cheese

2 eggs, beaten

4 tablespoons all-purpose flour

vegetable oil, for frying

salt and ground black pepper

For the chili jam

5 tablespoons olive oil

4 large onions, diced

4 garlic cloves, chopped

1–2 green chiles, seeded and sliced

2 tablespoons dark brown sugar

2 Let the onion mixture cool,
then transfer to a food
processor or blender. Add the
chiles and sugar and blend until
smooth, then return the mixture to
the saucepan. Cook for another
10 minutes, stirring frequently,
until the liquid evaporates and the
mixture has the consistency of
jam. Cool slightly.

3 To make the fritters, squeeze
the zucchini in a dish towel to
remove any excess liquid, then
combine with the Parmesan, eggs,
flour and salt and pepper.

4 Heat enough oil to cover the
bottom of a large frying pan.
Add 2 tablespoons of the mixture
for each fritter and cook three
fritters at a time. Cook for 2–3
minutes on each side, until golden,
then keep warm while you cook
the rest of the fritters. Drain on
paper towels and serve warm with
a spoonful of the chili jam.

1 First, make the chili jam. Heat
the oil in a frying pan until
hot, then add the onions and the
garlic. Reduce the heat to low, then
cook for 20 minutes, stirring
frequently, until the onions are
very soft.

COOK'S TIP

Stored in an airtight jar in the
refrigerator, the chili jam will
keep for up to 1 week

Charred Artichokes with Lemon Oil Dip

Here is a lip-smacking change from traditional fare.

INGREDIENTS

Serves 4

1 tablespoon lemon juice or white
   wine vinegar

2 artichokes, trimmed

12 garlic cloves, unpeeled

6 tablespoons olive oil

1 lemon

sea salt

flat-leaf parsley sprigs, to garnish

1 Preheat the oven to 400°F. Add the lemon juice or vinegar to a bowl of cold water. Cut each artichoke into wedges. Pull the hairy choke out from the center of each wedge and discard, then drop the wedges into the water.

2 Drain the wedges and place in a roasting pan with the garlic and 3 tablespoons of the oil. Toss well to coat. Sprinkle with salt and roast for 40 minutes, until tender and a little charred.

COOK'S TIP
~

Artichokes are usually boiled, but dry-heat cooking also works very well. If you can get young artichokes, try roasting them on a grill.

3 Meanwhile, make the dip. Using a small, sharp knife thinly pare away two strips of zest from the lemon. Lay the strips of zest on a board and carefully scrape off any remaining pith. Place the zest in a small pan with water to cover. Bring to a boil, then simmer for 5 minutes. Drain the zest, refresh in cold water, then chop coarsely. Set aside.

4 Arrange the cooked artichokes on a serving plate and let cool for 5 minutes. Using the back of a fork gently flatten the garlic cloves so that the flesh squeezes out of the skins. Transfer the garlic flesh to a bowl, mash into a paste, then add the lemon zest. Squeeze the juice from the lemon, then, using the fork, whisk the remaining olive oil and the lemon juice into the garlic mixture. Garnish with the parsley. Serve the artichokes still warm with the lemon oil dip.

Sesame Seed-coated Falafel with Tahini dip

Sesame seeds are used to give a delightfully crunchy coating to these spicy chickpea patties. Serve with the tahini yogurt dip, and some warmed pita bread too, if desired.

INGREDIENTS

Serves 6

1⅓ cups dried chickpeas

2 garlic cloves, crushed

1 red chile, seeded and finely sliced

1 teaspoon ground coriander

1 teaspoon ground cumin

1 tablespoon chopped fresh mint

1 tablespoon chopped fresh parsley

2 scallions, finely chopped

1 large egg, beaten

sesame seeds, for coating

sunflower oil, for frying

salt and ground black pepper

For the tahini yogurt dip

2 tablespoons light tahini

scant 1 cup plain yogurt

1 teaspoon cayenne pepper, plus extra for sprinkling

1 tablespoon chopped fresh mint

1 scallion, finely sliced

fresh herbs, to garnish

1 Place the chickpeas in a bowl, cover with cold water and let soak overnight. Drain and rinse the chickpeas, then place in a saucepan and cover with cold water. Bring to a boil and boil rapidly for 10 minutes. Reduce the heat; simmer for 1½–2 hours, until tender.

2 Meanwhile, make the tahini yogurt dip. Combine the tahini, yogurt, cayenne pepper and mint in a small bowl. Sprinkle the scallion and extra cayenne pepper on top and chill in the refrigerator until needed.

3 Combine the chickpeas with the garlic, chili, ground spices, herbs, scallions and seasoning, then mix in the egg. Place in a food processor and blend until the mixture forms a coarse paste. If the paste seems too soft, chill it for 30 minutes.

4 Form the chilled chickpea paste into 12 patties with your hands, then roll each one in the sesame seeds to coat thoroughly.

5 Heat enough oil to cover the bottom of a large frying pan Fry the falafel, in batches if necessary, for 6 minutes, turning once. Serve with the tahini yogurt dip garnished with fresh herbs.

Deep-fried New Potatoes with Saffron Aïoli

Serve these crispy little golden potatoes dipped into a garlicky mayonnaise—then sit back and watch them disappear in a matter of minutes!

Serves 4

1 egg yolk

½ teaspoon Dijon mustard

1¼ cups extra virgin olive oil

1–2 tablespoons lemon juice

1 garlic clove, crushed

½ teaspoon saffron threads

20 baby, new or salad potatoes

vegetable oil, for deep-frying

salt and ground black pepper

1 For the saffron aïoli, put the egg yolk in a bowl with the Dijon mustard and a pinch of salt. Stir to combine well. Beat in the olive oil very slowly, drop by drop at first and then in a very thin stream. Stir in the lemon juice.

2 Season the aïoli with salt and pepper, then add the crushed garlic and beat into the mixture thoroughly to combine.

3 Place the saffron in a small bowl and add 2 teaspoons hot water. Press the saffron with the back of a teaspoon, to extract the color and flavor, and let infuse for 5 minutes. Beat the saffron and the liquid into the aïoli.

4 Cook the potatoes in their skins in boiling salted water for 5 minutes, then turn off the heat. Cover the pan and leave for 15 minutes. Drain the potatoes, then dry them thoroughly in a dish towel.

5 Heat a ½-inch layer of vegetable oil in a deep pan. When the oil is very hot, add the potatoes and fry quickly, turning them constantly, until crisp and golden all over. Drain on paper towels and serve hot with the saffron aïoli.

Leek and Onion Tartlets

Baking in individual pans makes for easier serving for an appetizer and it looks attractive too. You could make tiny tartlets for parties.

INGREDIENTS

Serves 6

2 tablespoons butter

1 onion, thinly sliced

½ teaspoon dried thyme

1 pound leeks, thinly sliced

2 ounces Gruyère or Emmenthal
  cheese, grated

3 eggs

1¼ cups light cream

pinch of freshly grated nutmeg

salt and ground black pepper

mixed salad leaves, to serve

For the pastry

1⅓ cup all-purpose flour

6 tablespoons cold butter

1 egg yolk

2–3 tablespoons cold water

½ teaspoon salt

1 To make the pastry, sift the flour into a bowl and add the butter. Using your fingertips, rub the butter into the flour until it resembles fine bread crumbs. Make a well in the center of the mixture.

2 Beat together the egg yolk, water and salt, pour into the well and combine the flour and liquid until it begins to stick together. Form into a ball. Wrap and chill for 30 minutes.

3 Butter six 4-inch tartlet pans. On a lightly floured surface, roll out the dough until ⅛ inch thick, then using a 5-inch cutter, cut as many rounds as possible. Gently ease the rounds into the pans, pressing the pastry firmly into the bottom and sides. Re-roll the trimmings and line the remaining pans. Prick the bottoms all over and chill in the refrigerator for 30 minutes.

4 Preheat the oven to 375°F. Line the pastry crusts with aluminum foil and fill with baking beans. Place on a baking sheet and bake for 6–8 minutes, until golden at the edges. Remove the foil and beans and bake for another 2 minutes, until the bottoms appear dry. Transfer to a wire rack to cool. Reduce the oven temperature to 350°F.

5 In a large frying pan, melt the butter over medium heat, then add the onion and thyme and cook for 3–5 minutes, until the onion is just softened, stirring frequently. Add the thinly sliced leeks and cook for 10–12 minutes, until they are soft and tender, stirring occasionally. Divide the leek mixture among the pastry crusts and sprinkle each with cheese, dividing it evenly.

6 In a medium bowl, beat the eggs, cream, nutmeg and salt and pepper. Place the pastry crusts on a baking sheet and pour in the egg mixture. Bake for 15–20 minutes, until set and golden. Transfer the tartlets to a wire rack to cool slightly, then remove them from the pans and serve warm or at room temperature with salad leaves.

Chive Scrambled Eggs in Brioches

This is an indulgent, truly delicious and slightly quirky start to a meal— quick and easy too.

Serves 4

½ cup unsalted butter

generous 1 cup brown cap mushrooms, finely sliced

4 individual brioches

8 eggs

1 tablespoon snipped fresh chives, plus extra to garnish

salt and ground black pepper

1 Preheat the oven to 350°F. Place a quarter of the butter in a frying pan and heat until melted. Fry the mushrooms for about 3 minutes or until soft, then set aside and keep warm.

2 Slice the tops off the brioches, then scoop out the centers and discard. Put the brioches and lids on a baking sheet and bake for 5 minutes, until they are hot and slightly crisp.

3 Meanwhile, beat the eggs lightly and season to taste. Heat the remaining butter in a heavy saucepan over low heat. When the butter has melted and is foaming slightly, add the eggs. Using a wooden spoon, stir constantly to ensure that the egg does not stick.

4 Continue to stir gently until about three-quarters of the egg is semi-solid and creamy—this should take 2–3 minutes. Remove the pan from the heat—the egg will continue to cook in the heat from the pan—then stir in the snipped chives.

5 To serve, spoon a little of the mushrooms into the bottom of each brioche and top with the scrambled eggs. Sprinkle with extra chives, balance the brioche lids on top and serve immediately.

COOK'S TIP

Timing and temperature are crucial for perfect scrambled eggs. When cooked for too long over too high heat, eggs become dry and crumbly; if they are undercooked they will be sloppy and unappealing.

Risotto Frittata

*Half omelet, half risotto, this makes
a delightful and satisfying appetizer.
If possible, cook each frittata
separately, and preferably in a
small, cast-iron pan, so that the eggs
cook quickly underneath but stay
moist on top. Or cook in one large
pan and serve in wedges.*

INGREDIENTS

Serves 4

2–3 tablespoons olive oil

1 small onion, finely chopped

1 garlic clove, crushed

1 large red bell pepper, seeded and cut
    into thin strips

¾ cup risotto rice

1⅔–2 cups simmering vegetable stock

2–3 tablespoons butter

2½ cups button mushrooms, finely sliced

4 tablespoons freshly grated
    Parmesan cheese

6–8 eggs

salt and ground black pepper

1 Heat 1 tablespoon oil in a large
frying pan and fry the onion
and garlic over low heat for 2–3
minutes, until the onion begins to
soften but does not brown. Add
the pepper and cook, stirring, for
4–5 minutes, until soft.

2 Stir in the rice and cook gently
for 2–3 minutes, stirring
constantly, until the grains are
evenly coated with oil.

3 Add a quarter of the vegetable
stock and season with salt and
pepper. Stir over low heat until
the stock has been absorbed.
Continue to add more stock, a
little at a time, letting the rice
absorb the liquid before adding
more. Continue cooking in this
way until the rice is *al dente*.

4 In a separate small pan, heat a
little of the remaining oil and
some of the butter and quickly fry
the mushrooms until golden.
Transfer to a plate.

5 When the rice is tender,
remove from the heat and stir
in the cooked mushrooms and the
Parmesan cheese.

6 Beat together the eggs with
8 teaspoons cold water and
season well. Heat the remaining oil
and butter in an omelet pan and add
the risotto mixture. Spread the
mixture out in the pan, then
immediately add the beaten egg,
tilting the pan so that the omelet
cooks evenly. Fry over medium high
heat for 1–2 minutes, then transfer
to a warmed plate and serve.

COOK'S TIP

Don't be impatient while cooking
the rice. Adding the stock
gradually ensures a wonderfully
creamy consistency.

Pears and Stilton

Stilton is the classic British blue cheese, but you could use blue Cheshire instead, or even a non-British cheese such as Gorgonzola.

INGREDIENTS

Serves 4

4 ripe pears, lightly chilled

3 ounces blue Stilton

2 ounces cottage cheese

ground black pepper

watercress sprigs, to garnish

For the dressing

3 tablespoons light olive oil

1 tablespoon lemon juice

2 teaspoons toasted poppy seeds

salt and ground black pepper

1 First, make the dressing, place the olive oil and lemon juice, poppy seeds and seasoning in a screw-top jar and then shake together until emulsified.

2 Cut the pears in half lengthwise, then scoop out the cores and cut out the calyx from the rounded end.

3 Beat together the Stilton, curd cheese and a little pepper. Divide this mixture among the cavities in the pears.

4 Shake the dressing to mix it again, then spoon it on the pears. Serve garnished with some watercress sprigs.

COOK'S TIP

Comice pears are a good choice for this dish, being very juicy and aromatic. For a dramatic color contrast, select the excellent sweet and juicy Red Williams.

Vegetable Tempura

Tempura is a Japanese type of savory fritter. Originally shrimp were used, but vegetables can be cooked in the egg batter successfully too. The secret of making the incredibly light batter is to use really cold water and to have the oil at the right temperature before you start cooking the fritters.

INGREDIENTS

Serves 4

2 zucchini

½ eggplant

1 large carrot

½ small Spanish onion

1 egg

½ cup ice water

1 cup all-purpose flour

salt and ground black pepper

vegetable oil, for deep-frying

sea salt flakes, lemon slices and Japanese
    soy sauce (*shoyu*), to serve

1 Using a potato peeler, pare strips of peel from the zucchini and eggplant to give a striped effect.

2 Using a chef's knife, cut the zucchini, eggplant and carrot into strips measuring about 3–4 inches long and ⅛ inch wide. Place in a colander and sprinkle with salt. Put a small plate on top and weight it down. Leave for 30 minutes, then rinse. Drain then dry with paper towels.

3 Thinly slice the onion from top to bottom, discarding the plump pieces in the middle. Separate the layers so that there are lots of fine, long strips. Mix all the vegetables and season with salt and pepper.

4 Make the batter immediately before frying. Mix the egg and ice water in a bowl, then sift in the flour. Mix briefly with a fork or chopsticks. Do not overmix: the batter should remain lumpy. Add the vegetables to the batter and mix to combine.

5 Half-fill a wok with oil and heat to 350°F. Scoop up a heaping tablespoonful of the mixture at a time and carefully lower it into the oil. Deep-fry in batches for about 3 minutes, until golden brown and crisp. Drain on paper towels.

6 Serve each portion with salt, slices of lemon and a tiny bowl of Japanese soy sauce for dipping.

COOK'S TIP

Other suitable vegetables for tempura include mushrooms and slices of red, green, yellow or orange bell peppers.

Tortilla Wrap with Tabbouleh & Avocado

To be successful, tabbouleh needs scallions, lemon juice, plenty of fresh herbs and lots of freshly ground black pepper. It is best served at room temperature and goes very well with the chile and avocado mixture.

INGREDIENTS

Serves 6

1 cup bulghur wheat

2 tablespoons chopped fresh mint

2 tablespoons chopped fresh flat-
   leaf parsley

1 bunch scallions (about 6), sliced

½ cucumber, diced

¼ cup extra virgin olive oil

juice of 1 large lemon

salt and freshly ground black pepper

1 ripe avocado, pitted, peeled and diced

juice of ½ lemon

½ red chile, seeded and sliced

1 garlic clove, crushed

½ red bell pepper, seeded and finely diced

4 wheat tortillas, to serve

flat-leaf parsley, to garnish (optional)

1 To make the tabbouleh, place the bulghur wheat in a large heatproof bowl and pour in enough boiling water to cover. Leave for 30 minutes until the grains are tender but still retain a little resistance to the bite. Drain thoroughly in a sieve, then put back in the bowl.

2 Add the mint, parsley, scallions and cucumber to the bulghur wheat and mix thoroughly. Blend together the olive oil and lemon juice and pour onto the tabbouleh, season to taste and toss well to mix. Chill for 30 minutes to let the flavors mingle.

COOK'S TIP

The soaking time for bulghur wheat can vary. For the best results, follow the instructions on the package and taste the grain every now and again to check whether it is tender enough.

3 To make the avocado mixture, place the avocado in a bowl and add the lemon juice, chile and garlic. Season to taste and mash with a fork to form a smooth purée. Stir in the red bell pepper.

4 Warm the tortillas in a dry frying pan and serve either flat, folded or rolled up with the tabbouleh and avocado mixture. Garnish with parsley, if using.

Indian Mee Goreng

This colorful noodle dish is truly international, combining Indian, Chinese and Western ingredients. In Singapore and Malaysia it can be bought in many streets from one of the numerous hawkers' stalls.

INGREDIENTS

Serves 6

1 pound fresh yellow egg noodles

4–6 tablespoons vegetable oil

4 ounces fried tofu

2 eggs

2 tablespoons water

1 onion sliced

1 garlic clove, crushed

1 tablespoon light soy sauce

2–3 tablespoons ketchup

1 tablespoon chili sauce (or to taste)

1 large cooked potato, diced

4 scallions, shredded

1–2 fresh green chiles, seeded and finely
  sliced (optional)

1 Bring a large saucepan of water to a boil, add the fresh egg noodles and cook for just 2 minutes. Drain the noodles and immediately rinse them under cold water to stop them cooking. Drain again and set aside.

2 Cut each fried tofu cube in half, refresh it in a pan of boiling water, then drain well. Heat 2 tablespoons of the oil in a large frying pan. If using plain tofu, cut into cubes and fry until brown, then lift it out with a slotted spoon and set aside.

3 Beat the eggs with the water and seasoning. Add to the oil in the frying pan and cook without stirring until set. Flip over, cook the other side , then slide it out of the pan, roll up and slice thinly.

4 Heat the remaining oil in a wok and fry the onion and garlic for 2-3 minutes. Add the drained noodles, soy sauce, ketchup and chili sauce. Toss well over medium heat for 2 minutes, then add the diced potato. Reserve a few scallions for the garnish and stir the rest into the noodles with the chile, if using, and the tofu.

5 When hot , stir in the omelet. Serve on a hot platter garnished with the remaining scallions.

Twice-baked Gruyère and Potato Soufflé

A great appetizer dish, this recipe can be prepared in advance if you are entertaining and given its second baking just before you serve it.

Serves 4

8 ounces floury potatoes

2 eggs, separated

1½ cups Gruyère, grated

½ cup self-rising flour

2 ounces spinach leaves

butter, for greasing

salt and ground black pepper

salad greens, to serve

3 Finely chop the spinach and fold into the potato mixture.

4 Whip the egg whites until they form soft peaks. Fold a little of the egg white into the mixture to slacken it slightly. Using a large spoon, fold the remaining egg white into the mixture.

5 Grease 4 large ramekins. Pour the mixture into the dishes; place on a baking sheet. Bake for 20 minutes. Remove from the oven and let cool.

6 Turn the soufflés out onto a baking sheet and sprinkle on the remaining cheese. Bake again for 5 minutes; serve with salad greens.

1 Preheat the oven to 400°F. Peel the potatoes and cook in lightly salted boiling water for 20 minutes, until very tender. Drain and mash with the egg yolks.

2 Stir in half of the Gruyère cheese and all of the flour. Season to taste with salt and ground black pepper.

VARIATION

For a different flavoring try replacing the Gruyère with a crumbled blue cheese, such as Stilton or Shropshire Blue, which have a stronger taste.

Fried Rice Balls Stuffed with Mozzarella

These deep-fried balls of risotto go by the name of Suppli al Telefono in their native Italy. Stuffed with mozzarella cheese, they are very popular snacks, which is hardly surprising, as they are quite delicious. They make a wonderful start to any meal.

INGREDIENTS

Serves 4

1 batch Risotto alla Milanese, made without the saffron and with vegetable stock (see page 126)

3 eggs

bread crumbs and all-purpose flour, to coat

⅔ cup mozzarella cheese, cut into small cubes

oil, for deep-frying

dressed chicory and cherry tomatoes, to serve

1 Put the risotto in a bowl and let it cool completely. Beat two of the eggs, and stir them into the cooled risotto until well mixed.

2 Use your hands to form the rice mixture into balls the size of a large egg. If the mixture is too moist to hold its shape well, stir in a few spoonfuls of bread crumbs. Poke a hole in the center of each ball with your finger, then fill it with small cubes of mozzarella, and close the hole over again with the rice mixture.

COOK'S TIP

These provide the perfect solution as to what to do with leftover risotto, as they are best made with cold leftovers, cooked the day before.

3 Heat the oil for deep-frying until a small piece of bread sizzles as soon as it is dropped in.

4 Spread some flour on a plate. Beat the remaining egg in a shallow bowl. Sprinkle another plate with bread crumbs. Roll the balls in the flour, then in the egg, and finally in the bread crumbs.

5 Fry the rice balls, a few at a time, in the hot oil until golden and crisp. Drain on paper towels while the remaining balls are being fried and keep warm. Serve immediately, with a simple salad of dressed chicory leaves and cherry tomatoes.

Mini Baked Potatoes with Blue Cheese

These miniature potatoes can be eaten with your hands. They provide a great way of starting off an informal dinner party.

INGREDIENTS

Makes 20

20 small new or salad potatoes

4 tablespoons vegetable oil

coarse salt

½ cup sour cream

1 ounce blue cheese, crumbled

2 tablespoons snipped fresh chives,
   to garnish

1 Preheat the oven to 350°F. Wash and dry the potatoes. Toss with the oil in a bowl to coat.

2 Dip the potatoes in the coarse salt to coat lightly. Spread the potatoes out on a baking sheet. Bake for 45–50 minutes, until the potatoes are tender.

3 In a small bowl, combine the sour cream and blue cheese, mixing together well.

COOK'S TIP
~

This dish works just as well as a light snack; if you don't want to be bothered with lots of small potatoes, simply use an ordinary baking potato.

4 Cut a cross in the top of each potato. Press gently with your fingers to open the potatoes.

5 Top each potato with a dollop of the blue cheese mixture. Place on a serving dish and garnish with the chives. Serve hot or at room temperature.

Buckwheat Blinis with Mushroom Caviar

These little Russian pancakes are traditionally served with fish roe caviar and sour cream. Here is a vegetarian alternative that uses a selection of delicious wild mushrooms instead of the fish roe. The blinis can be made ahead of time and warmed before topping.

INGREDIENTS

Serves 4

1 cup bread flour

⅓ cup buckwheat flour

½ teaspoon salt

1¼ cups milk

1 teaspoon dried yeast

2 eggs, separated

scant 1 cup sour cream or crème fraîche

For the caviar

12 ounces mixed wild mushrooms such as field mushrooms, orange birch bolete, bay boletus, oyster and St. George's mushrooms

1 teaspoon celery salt

2 tablespoons walnut oil

1 tablespoon lemon juice

3 tablespoons chopped fresh parsley

ground black pepper

1 To make the caviar, trim and chop the mushrooms, then place them in a glass bowl, toss with the celery salt and cover with a weighted plate.

2 Leave the mushrooms for 2 hours, until the juices have run out into the bottom of the bowl. Rinse the mushrooms thoroughly to remove the salt, drain and press out as much liquid as you can with the back of a spoon. Return them to the bowl and toss with walnut oil, lemon juice, parsley and a twist of pepper. Chill in the refrigerator until ready to serve.

3 Sift the two flours together with the salt in a large mixing bowl. Gently warm the milk to about 98°. Add the yeast, stirring until dissolved, then pour into the flour, add the egg yolks and stir to make a smooth batter. Cover with a clean damp dish towel and set in a warm place for 1 hour.

4 Whisk the egg whites in a clean grease-free bowl until stiff then fold into the risen batter.

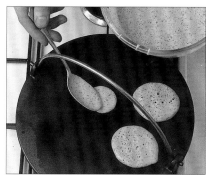

5 Heat griddle. Moisten with oil, then drop spoonfuls of the batter onto the surface. When bubbles rise to the surface, turn them over and cook briefly on the other side. Spoon on the sour cream or crème fraîche, top with the mushroom caviar and serve.

FAMILY
FAVORITES

Eggs Benedict

There is still debate over who created this recipe, but the most likely story credits a Mr. and Mrs. LeGrand Benedict, regulars at New York's Delmonico's restaurant, who complained there was nothing new on the lunch menu. This dish was created as a result.

INGREDIENTS

Serves 4

1 teaspoon vinegar

4 eggs

2 English muffins or 4 rounds of bread

butter, for spreading

4 thick slices cooked ham, trimmed to fit the muffins

fresh chives, to garnish

For the sauce

3 egg yolks

2 tablespoons fresh lemon juice

¼ teaspoon salt

½ cup butter

2 tablespoons light cream

ground black pepper

1 To make the sauce, blend the egg yolks, lemon juice, and salt in a food processor or blender for 15 seconds.

2 Melt the butter in a small saucepan until it bubbles (do not let it brown). With the motor running, pour the hot butter into the food processor through the feed tube in a slow, steady stream. Turn off the machine as soon as all the butter has been added.

3 Scrape the sauce into the top of a double boiler, over just simmering water. Stir for 2–3 minutes, until thickened. (If it curdles, whisk in 1 tablespoon boiling water.) Stir in the cream and season with pepper. Keep warm over the hot water.

4 Bring a shallow pan of water to a boil. Stir in the vinegar. Break each egg into a cup or bowl, then slide it carefully into the water. Carefully and gently turn the white around the yolk with a slotted spoon. Cook until the egg is set to your taste, about 3–4 minutes. Remove from the pan and place on paper towels to drain. Very gently cut any ragged edges off the eggs with a small knife or scissors.

5 While the eggs are poaching, split and toast the muffins or toast the bread slices. Butter while they are still warm.

6 Place a piece of ham, which you may brown in butter if desired, on each muffin half or slice of toast. Place an egg on each ham-topped muffin. Spoon the warm sauce over the eggs, garnish with chives and serve.

COOK'S TIP

For a special treat grate a little white or black truffle on top before serving.

Three-color Fish Kebabs

Don't let the fish marinate for more than an hour. The lemon juice will start to break down the fibers of the fish after this time, and it will then be difficult to avoid overcooking it.

INGREDIENTS

Serves 4

½ cup olive oil

finely grated zest and juice of
   1 large lemon

1 teaspoon crushed chile flakes

12 ounces monkfish fillet, cubed

12 ounces swordfish fillet, cubed

12 ounces thick salmon fillet or
   steak, cubed

2 red, yellow or orange bell peppers,
   cored, seeded and cut into squares

2 tablespoons finely chopped fresh
   flat-leaf parsley

salt and ground black pepper

For the sweet tomato and chili salsa

8 ounces ripe tomatoes, finely chopped

1 garlic clove, crushed

1 fresh red chile, seeded and chopped

3 tablespoons extra virgin olive oil

1 tablespoon lemon juice

1 tablespoon finely chopped fresh
   flat-leaf parsley

pinch of sugar

1 Put the oil in a shallow glass or china bowl and add the lemon zest and juice, the chile flakes and pepper to taste. Whisk to combine, then add the fish chunks. Turn to coat evenly.

2 Add the pepper squares, stir, then cover and marinate in a cool place for 1 hour, turning occasionally with a slotted spoon.

3 Thread the fish and peppers onto eight oiled metal skewers, reserving the marinade. Grill or broil the skewered fish for 5–8 minutes, turning once.

4 Meanwhile, make the salsa by mixing all the ingredients in a bowl, and seasoning to taste with salt and pepper. Heat the reserved marinade in a small pan, remove from the heat and stir in the parsley, with salt and pepper to taste. Serve the kebabs hot, with the marinade spooned on top, accompanied by the salsa.

> ### COOK'S TIP
> ∽
> Use tuna instead of swordfish, if desired. It has a similar meaty texture and will be equally successful.

Risotto Alla Milanese

This classic risotto is often served with the hearty beef stew, osso buco, but it also makes a delicious first course in its own right.

INGREDIENTS

Serves 5–6

about 5 cups beef or chicken stock

good pinch of saffron threads

6 tablespoons butter

1 onion, finely chopped

1½ cups risotto rice

1 cup freshly grated Parmesan cheese

salt and ground black pepper

1 Bring the stock to a boil, then reduce to a low simmer. Ladle a little stock into a small bowl. Add the saffron threads and let infuse.

2 Melt 4 tablespoons of the butter in a large saucepan until foaming. Add the onion and cook gently for about 3 minutes, stirring frequently, until softened but not browned at all.

3 Add the rice. Stir until the grains start to swell and burst, then add a few ladlefuls of the stock, with the saffron liquid and salt and pepper to taste. Stir over low heat until the stock has been absorbed. Add the remaining stock, a few ladlefuls at a time, letting the rice absorb all the liquid before adding more, and stirring constantly. After about 20–25 minutes, the rice should be just tender and the risotto golden yellow, moist and creamy.

4 Gently stir in about two-thirds of the grated Parmesan and the remaining butter. Heat through until the butter has melted, then taste for seasoning. Transfer the risotto to a warmed serving bowl or platter and serve hot, with the remaining grated Parmesan passed separately.

Hard-boiled Eggs with Tuna Sauce

The combination of eggs with a tasty tuna sauce makes a nourishing first course that is quick and easy to prepare.

Serves 6

6 extra large eggs

7-oumce can tuna in olive oil

3 anchovy fillets

1 tablespoon capers, drained

lemon juice

2 tablespoons olive oil

salt and ground black pepper

drained capers and anchovy fillets, to
    garnish (optional)

For the mayonnaise

1 egg yolk, at room temperature

1 teaspoon Dijon mustard

1 teaspoon white wine vinegar or
    lemon juice

⅔ cup olive oil

1 Boil the extra large eggs for
12–14 minutes. Drain under
cold water. Peel carefully and
set aside.

2 Make the mayonnaise by
whisking the egg yolk, mustard
and white wine vinegar or lemon
juice together in a small bowl.
Whisk in the oil a few drops at a
time, until 3–4 tablespoons oil
have been incorporated. Pour in
the remaining oil in a slow stream,
whisking constantly.

3 Place the tuna with its oil, the
anchovies, capers, lemon juice
and olive oil in a blender or a food
processor. Process until smooth.

4 Fold the tuna sauce into the
mayonnaise. Season with black
pepper and extra salt if necessary.
Chill for at least 1 hour.

5 To serve, cut the eggs in half
lengthwise. Arrange them on a
serving platter. Spoon on the
sauce, and garnish with capers and
anchovy fillets, if using. Serve the
eggs chilled.

Spinach Empanadillas

These are little pastry turnovers, filled with ingredients that have a strong Moorish influence—pine nuts and raisins. Serve with pre-dinner drinks at an informal dinner party, allowing two to three per person.

INGREDIENTS

Makes 20

2 tablespoons raisins

1½ tablespoons olive oil

1 pound fresh spinach, washed and chopped

6 drained canned anchovies, chopped

2 garlic cloves, finely chopped

⅓ cup pine nuts, chopped

1 egg, beaten

12 ounces puff pastry

salt and ground black pepper

1 To make the filling, soak the raisins in a little warm water for 10 minutes. Drain, then chop roughly. Heat the oil in a large sauté pan or wok, add the spinach, stir, then cover and cook over low heat for about 2 minutes. Uncover, turn up the heat and let any liquid evaporate. Add the anchovies, garlic and seasoning, then cook, stirring, for another minute. Remove from heat, add the raisins and pine nuts, and cool.

2 Preheat the oven to 350°F. Roll out the pastry to a ⅛ inch thickness.

3 Using a 3-inch pastry cutter, cut out 20 rounds, re-rolling the dough if necessary. Place about two teaspoonfuls of the filling in the middle of each round, then brush the edges with a little water. Bring up the sides of the pastry and seal well.

4 Press the edges of the pastry together with the back of a fork. Brush with beaten egg. Place the turnovers on a lightly greased baking sheet and bake for about 15 minutes, until golden. Serve the empanadillas warm.

Thai-style Seafood Dumplings

These elegant appetizer-size dumplings are filled with fish, shrimp and Thai fragrant rice, and are subtly flavored with fresh cilantro, garlic and ginger.

INGREDIENTS

Makes 18

all-purpose flour, for dusting

1¼ pounds puff pastry, thawed if frozen

1 egg, beaten with 2 tablespoons water

lime twists, to garnish

For the filling

10 ounces skinned white fish fillets, such as cod or haddock

seasoned all-purpose flour

8–10 large raw shrimp

1 tablespoon sunflower oil

about 6 tablespoons butter

6 scallions, finely sliced

1 garlic clove, crushed

2 cups cooked Thai fragrant rice

1½-inch piece fresh ginger, grated

2 teaspoons finely chopped fresh cilantro

1 teaspoon finely grated lime zest

1 Preheat the oven to 375°F. Make the filling. Cut the fish into ¾-inch cubes and dust with seasoned flour. Peel and devein the shrimp and cut each one into four pieces.

2 Heat half of the oil and 1 tablespoon of the butter in a frying pan. Fry the scallions gently for 2 minutes.

3 Add the garlic and fry for another 5 minutes, until the onions are very soft. Transfer to a large bowl.

4 Heat the remaining oil and another 2 tablespoons of the butter in a clean pan. Fry the fish pieces briefly. As soon as they begin to turn opaque, use a slotted spoon to transfer them to the bowl with the scallions. Cook the shrimp in the fat remaining in the pan. When they begin to change color, lift them out and add them to the bowl.

5 Add the cooked rice to the bowl, with the fresh ginger, cilantro and grated lime zest. Mix, being careful not to break up the fish.

6 Dust the work surface with a little flour. Roll out the pastry and cut into 4-inch rounds. Place spoonfuls of filling just off center on the pastry rounds. Dot with a little of the remaining butter. Dampen the edges of the pastry with a little of the egg wash, fold one side of the pastry over the filling and press the edges together firmly.

7 Place the dumplings on two lightly greased baking sheets. Decorate them with the pastry trimmings, if desired, and brush them with egg wash. Bake for 12–15 minutes or until golden brown all over.

8 Transfer to a plate and garnish with lime twists.

Fish Sausages

This recipe originated in Hungary during the seventeenth century. It is still popular today.

INGREDIENTS

Serves 4

13 ounces fish fillets, such as perch, pike, carp or cod, skinned

1 white-bread roll

5 tablespoons milk

1½ tablespoons chopped fresh flat- leaf parsley

2 eggs, well beaten

½ cup all-purpose flour

1 cup fine fresh white bread crumbs

oil, for shallow frying

salt and ground black pepper

deep-fried parsley sprigs and lemon wedges, dusted with paprika, to garnish

1 Grind or process the fish coarsely in a food processor or blender. Soak the roll in the milk for about 10 minutes, then squeeze it out. Combine the fish and bread before adding the chopped parsley, one of the eggs and plenty of seasoning.

2 Using your fingers, shape the fish mixture into 4-inch long sausages, making them about 1-inch thick.

3 Carefully roll the fish "sausages" in the flour, then in the remaining egg and finally in the bread crumbs.

4 Heat the oil in a pan then slowly cook the "sausages," until golden brown all over. (You may need to work in batches.) Drain well on crumpled paper towels. Garnish with the deep-fried parsley sprigs and lemon wedges dusted with paprika.

Deep-fried Whitebait

A spicy coating on these fish gives this favorite dish a crunchy bite.

Serves 6

1 cup all-purpose flour

½ teaspoon curry powder

½ teaspoon ground ginger

½ teaspoon ground cayenne pepper

pinch of salt

2½ pounds whitebait, thawed if frozen

vegetable oil, for deep-frying

lemon wedges, to garnish

1 Combine the flour, curry powder, ground ginger, cayenne pepper and a little salt in a large bowl.

2 Coat the fish in the seasoned flour, covering them evenly.

3 Heat the oil in a large, heavy saucepan until it reaches a temperature of 375°F. Fry the whitebait in batches for 2–3 minutes, until the fish is golden and crispy.

4 Drain the whitebait well on paper towels. Keep warm in a low oven until you have cooked all the fish. Serve immediately, garnished with lemon wedges for squeezing on top.

Paella Croquettes

Paella is probably Spain's most famous dish, and here it is used for a tasty fried tapas. In this recipe, the paella is cooked from scratch, but you could, of course, use leftover paella instead.

INGREDIENTS

Serves 4

pinch of saffron threads

⅔ cup white wine

2 tablespoons olive oil

1 small onion, finely chopped

1 garlic clove, finely chopped

⅔ cup risotto rice

1¼ cups hot chicken stock

½ cup cooked shrimp, peeled, deveined
   and coarsely chopped

2 ounces cooked chicken, coarsely
   chopped

⅔ cup petits pois, thawed if frozen

2 tablespoons freshly grated
   Parmesan cheese

1 egg, beaten

2 tablespoons milk

1½ cups fresh white bread crumbs

vegetable or olive oil, for shallow-frying

salt and ground black pepper

flat-leaf parsley, to garnish

1 Stir the saffron into the wine in a small bowl; set aside.

2 Heat the oil in a saucepan and gently fry the onion and garlic for 5 minutes, until softened. Stir in the risotto rice and cook, stirring, for 1 minute.

3 Keeping the heat fairly high, add the wine and saffron mixture to the pan, stirring until it is all absorbed. Gradually add the stock, stirring until all the liquid has been absorbed and the rice is cooked—this should take about 20 minutes.

4 Stir in the shrimp, chicken, petits pois and freshly grated Parmesan. Season to taste. Let cool slightly, then use two tablespoons to shape the mixture into 16 small lozenges.

5 Mix the egg and milk in a shallow bowl. Spread out the bread crumbs on a sheet of foil. Dip the croquettes in the egg mixture, then coat them evenly in the bread crumbs.

6 Heat the oil in a large frying pan. Then shallow fry the croquettes for 4–5 minutes, until crisp and golden brown. Work in batches. Drain on paper towels and keep hot. Serve garnished with a sprig of flat-leaf parsley.

Herbed Plaice Fritters

Serve these baby croquettes with tartar sauce, if desired. Simply chop some capers and gherkins, and stir into homemade or good quality store-bought mayonnaise. Season to taste.

INGREDIENTS

Serves 4

1 pound plaice fillets

1¼ cups milk

1 pound cooked potatoes

1 fennel bulb, finely chopped

3 tablespoons chopped fresh parsley

2 eggs

1 tablespoon unsalted butter

2 cups white bread crumbs

2 tablespoons sesame seeds

oil, for deep-frying

salt and ground black pepper

1 Gently poach the plaice fillets in the milk for approximately 15 minutes, until the fish flakes. Drain and reserve the milk.

2 Peel the skin off the fish and remove any bones. In a food processor fitted with a metal blade, process the fish, potatoes, fennel, parsley, eggs and butter.

3 Add 2 tablespoons of the reserved cooking milk and season with salt and plenty of ground black pepper. Mix well. Chill for 30 minutes, then shape into twenty even-size croquettes with your hands.

4 Combine the bread crumbs and sesame seeds, then roll the croquettes in this mixture to form a good coating. Heat the oil in a large, heavy saucepan until it is hot enough to brown a cube of stale bread in 30 seconds. Deep-fry the croquettes in small batches for about 4 minutes, until they are golden brown all over. Drain well on paper towels and serve the fritters hot.

Thai Fish Cakes with Cucumber Relish

These wonderful small fish cakes are a very familiar and popular appetizer. They are usually accompanied with Thai beer, or choose a robust oaked Chardonnay instead.

INGREDIENTS

Makes about 12

11 ounces white fish fillet, such as cod, cut into chunks

2 tablespoons red curry paste

1 egg

2 tablespoons fish sauce

1 teaspoon granulated sugar

2 tablespoons cornstarch

3 kaffir lime leaves, shredded

1 tablespoon chopped fresh cilantro

2 ounces green beans, finely sliced

oil, for frying

watercress, to garnish

For the cucumber relish

4 tablespoons Thai rice vinegar

4 tablespoons water

2 ounces sugar

1 whole bulb pickled garlic

1 cucumber, quartered and sliced

4 shallots, finely sliced

1 tablespoon chopped fresh ginger

1 To make the cucumber relish, bring the vinegar, water and sugar to a boil. Stir until the sugar dissolves, then remove from the heat and let cool.

2 Combine the rest of the relish ingredients together in a bowl and pour in the vinegar mixture.

3 Combine the fish, curry paste and egg in a food processor and process well. Transfer the mixture to a bowl, add the rest of the ingredients, except the oil and garnish, and mix well.

4 Mold and shape the mixture into cakes about 2 inches in diameter and ¼ inch thick.

5 Heat the oil in a wok or deep-fat fryer. Fry the fish cakes, working in small batches, for 4–5 minutes or until golden brown. Remove and drain on paper towels. Keep warm in a low oven. Garnish with watercress and serve with a little cucumber relish spooned on the side.

Crab and Ricotta Tartlets

Use the meat from a freshly cooked crab, weighing about 1 pound, if you can. Otherwise, look for frozen brown and white crabmeat.

INGREDIENTS

Serves 4

2 cups all-purpose flour

pinch of salt

$\frac{1}{2}$ cup butter, diced

1 cup ricotta

1 tablespoon grated onion

2 tablespoons freshly grated
   Parmesan cheese

$\frac{1}{2}$ teaspoon mustard powder

2 eggs, plus 1 egg yolk

8 ounces crab meat

2 tablespoons chopped fresh parsley

$\frac{1}{2}$–1 teaspoon anchovy extract

1–2 teaspoons lemon juice

salt and cayenne pepper

salad greens, to garnish

1 Preheat the oven to 400°F. Sift the flour and salt into a bowl, add the butter and rub it in until the mixture resembles fine bread crumbs. Stir in about 4 tablespoons of cold water to make a firm dough.

2 Turn the dough onto a floured surface and knead lightly. Roll out the pastry and use to line four 4-inch tartlet pans. Prick the bottoms with a fork, then chill for 30 minutes.

3 Line the pastry shells with waxed paper and fill with baking beans. Bake for 10 minutes, then remove the paper and beans. Return to the oven and bake for another 10 minutes.

4 Place the ricotta, grated onion, Parmesan and mustard powder in a bowl and beat until soft. Gradually beat in the eggs and egg yolk.

5 Gently stir in the crab meat and chopped parsley, then add the anchovy extract, lemon juice, salt and cayenne pepper, to taste.

6 Remove the tartlet shells from the oven and reduce the temperature to 350°F. Spoon the filling into the shells and bake for 20 minutes, until set and golden brown. Serve hot with a garnish of salad greens.

Grilled Jumbo Shrimp with Romesco Sauce

This sauce, originally from the Catalan region of Spain, is served with fish and shellfish. Its main ingredients are sweet bell pepper, tomatoes, garlic and almonds.

INGREDIENTS

Serves 6–8

24 jumbo shrimp
2–3 tablespoons olive oil
flat-leaf parsley, to garnish
lemon wedges, to serve

For the sauce

2 well-flavored tomatoes
4 tablespoons olive oil
1 onion, chopped
4 garlic cloves, chopped
1 canned pimiento, chopped
½ teaspoon dried chili flakes or powder
5 tablespoons fish stock
2 tablespoons white wine
10 blanched almonds
1 tablespoon red wine vinegar
salt, to taste

3 Toast the almonds under the broiler until golden. Transfer to a blender or food processor and grind coarsely. Add the remaining 2 tablespoons of oil, the vinegar and the last garlic clove and process until evenly combined. Add the tomato and pimiento sauce and process until smooth. Season with salt, to taste.

4 Remove the heads from the shrimp, leaving them otherwise unpeeled and, with a sharp knife, slit each one down the back and remove the dark vein. Rinse and pat dry on paper towels. Preheat the broiler. Toss the shrimp in olive oil, then spread out in a broiler pan. Broil for 2–3 minutes on each side, until pink. Arrange on a serving platter with the lemon wedges, and the sauce in a small bowl. Serve immediately, garnished with parsley.

1 To make the sauce, immerse the tomatoes in boiling water for about 30 seconds, then refresh them under cold water. Peel off the skins and roughly chop the tomato flesh.

2 Heat 2 tablespoons of the oil in a pan, add the onion and 3 of the garlic cloves and cook until soft. Add the pimiento, tomatoes, chili, fish stock and wine, then cover and simmer for 30 minutes.

Breaded Sole Batons

Goujons of lemon sole are coated in seasoned flour and then in bread crumbs, and fried until deliciously crispy. They are served with piquant tartar sauce.

INGREDIENTS

Serves 4

10 ounces lemon sole fillets, skinned

2 eggs

1½ cups fine fresh bread crumbs

6 tablespoons all-prupose flour

salt and ground black pepper

vegetable oil, for frying

tartar sauce and lemon wedges, to serve

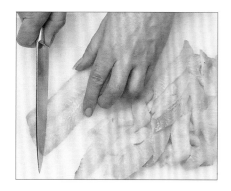

1 Cut the fish fillets into long diagonal strips about ¾ inch wide, using a sharp knife.

2 Break the eggs into a shallow dish and beat well with a fork. Place the bread crumbs in another shallow dish. Put the flour in a large plastic bag and season with salt and plenty of ground black pepper.

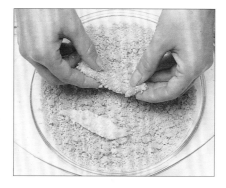

3 Dip the fish strips in the egg, turning to coat well. Place on a plate and then, taking a few at a time, shake them in the bag of flour. Dip the fish strips in the egg again, then in the bread crumbs, turning to coat well. Place on a tray in a single layer, not touching. Let the coating set for at least 10 minutes.

4 Heat ½ inch oil in a large frying pan over medium-high heat. When the oil is hot (a cube of bread will sizzle) fry the fish strips for 2–2½ minutes in batches, turning once, taking care not to overcrowd the pan. Drain on paper towels and keep warm. Serve the fish with tartar sauce and lemon wedges.

Salmon Cakes with Butter Sauce

Salmon fish cakes make a real treat for the start of a dinner party. They are also economical, as you could use any small tail pieces that are available at your local fishmonger or supermarket.

INGREDIENT

Makes 6

8 ounces salmon tail pieces, cooked

2 tablespoons chopped fresh parsley

2 scallions, trimmed and chopped

grated zest and juice of ½ lemon

8 ounces mashed potatoes (not too soft)

1 egg, beaten

1 cup fresh white bread crumbs

6 tablespoons butter, plus extra for frying (optional)

oil, for frying (optional)

salt and ground black pepper

zucchini and carrot slices and sprig of cilantro, to garnish

1 Remove all the skin and bones from the fish and mash or flake it well. Add the fresh parsley, onions and 1 teaspoon of the lemon zest, and season with salt and lots of black pepper.

2 Gently work in the potatoes, and then shape into six rounds, triangles or croquettes. Chill the salmon cakes for 20 minutes.

3 Preheat the broiler. When chilled, coat the salmon cakes well in egg and then in the bread crumbs. Broil gently for 5 minutes on each side or until they are golden, or fry in butter and oil.

4 To make the butter sauce, melt the butter, whisk in the remaining lemon zest, the lemon juice, 1–2 tablespoons water and seasoning to taste. Simmer for a few minutes and serve with the hot fish cakes. Garnish with slices of zucchini and carrot and a sprig of cilantro.

Italian Shrimp Skewers

Parsley and lemon are all that is needed to create a great shrimp dish. Broil them, or grill them for an informal al fresco *summer appetizer.*

INGREDIENTS

Serves 4

2 pounds tiger shrimp, peeled

4 tablespoons olive oil

3 tablespoons vegetable oil

1¼ cups very fine dry bread crumbs

1 garlic clove, crushed

1 tablespoon chopped fresh parsley

salt and ground black pepper

lemon wedges, to serve

1 Slit the shrimp down their backs and remove the dark vein. Rinse in cold water and pat dry on paper towels.

2 Put the olive oil and vegetable oil in a large bowl and add the shrimp, mixing them to coat evenly. Add the bread crumbs, garlic and parsley and season with salt and pepper. Toss the shrimp thoroughly, to give them an even coating of bread crumbs. Cover and marinate for 1 hour.

4 Preheat the broiler. Place the skewers in a broiler pan and cook for about 2 minutes on each side, until the bread crumbs are golden. Serve with lemon wedges.

3 Thread the tiger shrimp onto four metal or wooden skewers, curling them up as you work, so that the tails are skewered neatly in the middle.

Kansas City Fritters

These fritters are made wonderfully light by the egg whites, which are whisked separately before being folded in.

INGREDIENTS

Makes 8

1¼ cups canned sweetcorn, drained

2 eggs, separated

⅓ cup all-purpose flour

6 tablespoons milk

1 small zucchini, grated

2 strips bacon, diced

2 scallions, finely chopped

good pinch of cayenne pepper

3 tablespoons sunflower oil

salt and ground black pepper

cilantro sprigs, to garnish

For the salsa

3 tomatoes, peeled, seeded and diced

½ small red bell pepper, seeded and diced

½ small onion, diced

1 tablespoon lemon juice

1 tablespoon chopped fresh cilantro

dash of Tabasco sauce

1 To make the salsa, place all the ingredients in a bowl, mix well and season. Cover and chill.

2 Empty the corn into a large bowl and mix in the egg yolks. Add the flour and blend in with a wooden spoon. When the mixture begins to thicken, gradually blend in the milk.

3 Stir in the grated zucchini, bacon, scallions, cayenne pepper and seasoning and set aside until required.

4 Place the egg whites in a clean bowl and whisk until stiff. Gently fold into the corn batter mixture with a metal spoon.

5 Heat 2 tablespoons of the oil in a large frying pan and place four large spoonfuls of the mixture in the oil. Fry over medium heat for 2–3 minutes on each side until golden, then drain on paper towels. Keep warm in the oven while frying the remaining four fritters, adding the rest of the oil if necessary.

6 Serve two fritters each, garnished with cilantro sprigs and a spoonful of the chilled tomato salsa.

Chicken Croquettes

This recipe comes from Rebato's, a tapas bar in London. The chef there makes croquettes with a number of different flavorings; this version uses chicken.

INGREDIENTS

Serves 4

2 tablespoons butter

¼ cup all-purpose flour

⅔ cup milk

1 tablespoon olive oil

1 boneless chicken breast with skin, about 3 ounces, diced

1 garlic clove, finely chopped

1 small egg, beaten

1 cup fresh white bread crumbs

vegetable oil, for deep-frying

salt and ground black pepper

flat-leaf parsley, to garnish

lemon wedges, to serve

1 Melt the butter in a small saucepan. Add the flour and cook gently, stirring, for 1 minute. Gradually beat in the milk to make a smooth, very thick sauce. Cover with a lid and remove from the pan from the heat.

2 Heat the oil in a frying pan and cook the chicken with the garlic for 5 minutes, until the chicken is lightly browned and cooked through.

3 Turn the contents of the frying pan into a food processor or blender and process until finely chopped. Stir the chicken into the sauce, mixing it well. Add plenty of salt and pepper to taste. Let cool completely.

4 Shape into eight even-size sausages, then dip each in egg and then bread crumbs. Deep-fry in hot oil for 4 minutes, until crisp and golden. Drain on paper towels and serve garnished with parsley and lemon wedges for squeezing.

Chicken Bitki

This is a popular Polish dish and makes an attractive appetizer when offset by deep red beets and vibrant green salad greens.

INGREDIENTS

Makes 12

1 tablespoon butter, melted

4 ounces flat mushrooms, finely chopped

1 cup fresh white bread crumbs

12 ounces chicken breasts or guinea fowl, ground or finely chopped

2 eggs, separated

¼ teaspoon grated nutmeg

2 tablespoons all-purpose flour

3 tablespoons oil

salt and ground black pepper

salad greens and grated pickled beets, to serve

1 Melt the butter in a pan and fry the mushrooms for about 5 minutes, until soft and the juices have evaporated. Let cool.

2 Combine the mushrooms and the bread crumbs, the chicken or guinea fowl, egg yolks, nutmeg, salt and pepper.

3 Whisk the egg whites until stiff. Stir half into the chicken mixture to slacken it, then fold in the remainder.

4 Shape into 12 even-size meatballs, about 3 inches long and 1 inch wide. Roll in the flour to coat.

5 Heat the oil in a frying pan and fry the bitki for about 10 minutes, turning until evenly golden brown and cooked through. Serve hot with salad greens and pickled beets.

Chicken Parcels

These homemade chicken parcels look great piled high and golden brown.

Makes 35

2 cups all-purpose flour, plus extra for dusting

½ teaspoon salt

½ teaspoon sugar

1 teaspoon easy-blend dried yeast

2 tablespoons butter, softened

1 egg, beaten, plus a little extra

6 tablespoons warm milk

lemon wedges, to serve

For the filling

1 small onion, finely chopped

1½ cups ground chicken

1 tablespoon sunflower oil

5 tablespoons chicken stock

2 tablespoons chopped fresh parsley

pinch of grated nutmeg

salt and ground black pepper

1 Sift the flour, salt and sugar into a large bowl. Stir in the dried yeast, then make a well in the center of the flour.

2 Add the butter, egg and milk and mix into a soft dough. Turn onto a lightly floured surface and knead for 10 minutes, until the dough is smooth and elastic.

3 Put the dough in a clean bowl, cover with plastic wrap and then set in a warm place to rise for 1 hour or until the dough has doubled in size.

4 Meanwhile, fry the onion and chicken in the oil for about 10 minutes. Add the stock and simmer for 5 minutes. Stir in the parsley, grated nutmeg and salt and ground black pepper. Then let cool.

5 Preheat the oven to 425°F. Knead the dough, then roll it out until it is ⅛ inch thick. Stamp out rounds with a 3-inch cutter.

6 Brush the edges with beaten egg. Put a little filling in the middle, then press the edges together. Let rise on oiled baking sheets, covered with oiled plastic wrap, for 15 minutes. Brush with a little more egg. Bake for 5 minutes, then for 10 minutes at 375°F, until well risen. Serve with lemon wedges.

Stuffed Garlic Mushrooms with Prosciutto

Field mushrooms can vary greatly in size. Choose similar-size specimens with undamaged edges.

INGREDIENTS

Serves 4

1 onion, chopped

6 tablespoons unsalted butter

8 field mushrooms

¼ cup dried cêpes, bay boletus or saffron milk-caps, soaked in warm water for 20 minutes

1 garlic clove, crushed

¾ cup fresh bread crumbs

1 egg

5 tablespoons chopped fresh parsley

1 tablespoon chopped fresh thyme

salt and ground black pepper

4 ounces prosciutto di Parma or San Daniele, thinly sliced

fresh parsley, to garnish

1 Preheat the oven to 375°F. Fry the onion gently in half the butter for 6–8 minutes, until soft but not colored. Meanwhile, break off the stems of the field mushrooms, setting the caps aside. Drain the dried mushrooms and chop these and the stems of the field mushrooms finely. Add to the onion together with the garlic and cook for another 2–3 minutes.

2 Transfer the mixture to a bowl, add the bread crumbs, egg, herbs and seasoning. Melt the remaining butter in a small pan and generously brush onto the mushroom caps. Arrange the mushrooms on a baking sheet and spoon in the filling. Bake for 20–25 minutes, until they are well browned.

3 Top each mushroom with a slice of prosciutto, garnish with parsley and serve.

COOK'S TIP

• Garlic mushrooms can be easily prepared in advance ready to go into the oven.

• Fresh bread crumbs can be made and then frozen. They can be taken from the freezer as needed and do not need to be defrosted first.

Glazed Chicken Skewers

Known as Yakitori in Japan, these skewers are popular throughout the country and are often served as an appetizer with drinks.

Makes 12 skewers and 8 wing pieces

8 chicken wings

4 chicken thighs, skinned

4 scallions, blanched and cut into short lengths

For the basting sauce

4 tablespoons sake

⅓ cup dark soy sauce

2 tablespoons tamari sauce

1 tablespoon mirin, or sweet sherry

1 tablespoon sugar

1 Remove the wing tip of the chicken at the first joint. Chop through the second joint, revealing the two narrow bones. Take hold of the bones with a clean cloth and pull, turning the meat around the bones inside out. Remove the smaller bone and discard. Set the wings aside.

2 Bone the chicken thighs and cut the meat into large dice. Thread the scallions and thigh meat onto 12 skewers.

3 Measure the basting sauce ingredients into a stainless-steel or enamel saucepan and simmer until reduced by two-thirds. Cool.

4 Heat the broiler to medium high. Broil the skewers without applying any oil. When juices begin to emerge from the chicken, baste liberally with the sauce. Allow another 3 minutes for the chicken on skewers and not more than 5 minutes for the wings.

Pork Saté

Originating in Indonesia, saté are skewers of meat marinated with spices and grilled quickly over charcoal. It's street food at its best, prepared by vendors with portable grills who set up stalls at every road side and marketplace. It makes a great-tasting appetizer too. It's not too filling, and it's bursting with flavor. You can make saté with chicken, beef or lamb. Serve with saté sauce, and a cucumber relish, if desired.

INGREDIENTS

Makes about 20

1 pound lean pork

1 teaspoon grated fresh ginger

1 lemongrass stalk, finely chopped

3 garlic cloves, finely chopped

1 tablespoon medium curry paste

1 teaspoon ground cumin

1 teaspoon ground turmeric

4 tablespoons coconut cream

2 tablespoons fish sauce

1 teaspoon sugar

oil, for brushing

fresh herbs, to garnish

For the saté sauce

1 cup coconut milk

2 tablespoons red curry paste

3 ounces crunchy peanut butter

½ cup chicken stock

3 tablespoons brown sugar

2 tablespoons tamarind juice

1 tablespoon fish sauce

½ teaspoon salt

1 Cut the pork thinly into 2-inch strips. Combine the fresh ginger, lemongrass, garlic, curry paste, cumin, turmeric, coconut cream, fish sauce and sugar.

2 Pour on the pork and let marinate for about 2 hours.

3 Meanwhile, make the sauce. Heat the coconut milk over medium heat, then add the red curry paste, peanut butter, chicken stock and sugar.

4 Cook and stir until smooth, 5–6 minutes. Add the tamarind juice, fish sauce and salt to taste.

5 Thread the meat onto skewers. Brush with oil and grill over charcoal or under a preheated broiler for 3–4 minutes on each side, turning occasionally, until cooked and golden brown. Serve with the satay sauce garnished with fresh herbs.

Spicy Koftas

These koftas will need to be cooked in batches. Keep them hot when they are cooked while you cook the rest.

INGREDIENTS

Makes 20–25

1 pound lean ground beef or lamb

2 tablespoons finely ground ginger

2 tablespoons finely minced garlic

4 green chiles, finely chopped

1 small onion, finely chopped

1 egg

½ teaspoon turmeric

1 teaspoon garam masala

2 ounces cilantro leaves, chopped

4–6 mint leaves, chopped, or ½ teaspoon mint sauce

6 ounces raw potato

salt, to taste

vegetable oil, for deep-frying

1 Place the beef or lamb in a large bowl along with the ginger, garlic, chiles, onion, egg, spices and herbs. Grate the potato into the bowl, and season with salt. Knead to blend well and form a soft dough.

2 Using your fingers, shape the kofta mixture into portions the size of golf balls. You should be able to make 20 to 25 koftas. Let the balls rest at room temperature for about 25 minutes.

3 In a wok or frying pan, heat the oil to medium-hot and fry the koftas in small batches until they are golden brown in color. Drain well and serve hot.

COOK'S TIP

Leftover koftas can be coarsely chopped and packed into pita bread spread with chutney or relish for a quick and delicious snack.

Golden Parmesan Chicken

Served cold with the garlicky mayonnaise these morsels of chicken make a great appetizer, especially if served informally as finger food.

INGREDIENTS

Serves 4

4 chicken breast fillets, skinned

1½ cups fresh white bread crumbs

1½ ounces Parmesan cheese, finely grated

2 tablespoons chopped fresh parsley

2 eggs, beaten

½ cup good-quality mayonnaise

½ cup fromage frais

1–2 garlic cloves, crushed

4 tablespoons butter, melted

salt and ground black pepper

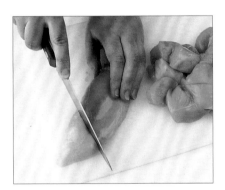

1 Cut each fillet into four or five chunks. Combine the bread crumbs, Parmesan, parsley and seasoning in a shallow dish.

2 Dip the chicken pieces in the egg, then into the bread crumb mixture. Place in a single layer on a baking sheet; chill for 30 minutes.

3 Meanwhile, to make the garlic mayonnaise, combine the mayonnaise, fromage frais and garlic, and season to taste with ground black pepper. Spoon the mayonnaise into a small serving bowl. Chill until needed.

4 Preheat the oven to 350°F. Drizzle the melted butter on the chicken pieces and cook them for about 20 minutes, until crisp and golden. Serve the chicken immediately, accompanied by the garlic mayonnaise for dipping.

Savory Pork Pies

These little pies come from Spain and are fun to eat.

Makes 12 pastries

Ingredients

12 ounces shortcrust pastry, thawed
   if frozen

For the filling

1 tablespoon vegetable oil

1 onion, chopped

1 clove garlic, crushed

1 teaspoon thyme

1 cup ground pork

1 teaspoon paprika

salt and ground black pepper

1 hard-boiled egg, chopped

1 gherkin, chopped

2 tablespoons chopped fresh parsley

vegetable oil, for deep-frying

1 To make the filling, heat the vegetable oil in a saucepan or wok and soften the onion, garlic and thyme without browning, for 3–4 minutes. Add the pork and paprika, then brown evenly for 6–8 minutes. Season well, turn out into a bowl and cool. When the mixture is cool, add the hard-boiled egg, gherkin and parsley.

2 Turn the pastry out onto a floured work surface and roll out to a 15-inch square. Cut out 12 circles 5 inches in diameter. Place 1 tablespoon of the filling on each circle, moisten the edges with a little water, fold over and seal.

3 Heat the vegetable oil in a deep-fryer fitted with a basket, to 385°F. Place three pies at a time in the basket and deep-fry until golden brown. Frying should take at least 1 minute or the inside filling will not be heated through. Serve warm in a basket covered with a napkin.

Deep-fried Lamb Patties

These patties are a tasty North African specialty—called kibbeh — of ground meat and bulghur wheat. They are sometimes stuffed with additional meat and deep-fried. Moderately spiced, they're good served with yogurt.

INGREDIENTS

Serves 6

1 pound lean lamb (or lean ground lamb or beef)
salt and ground black pepper
oil, for deep-frying
avocado slices and cilantro sprigs, to serve

For the patties
1⅓ cups bulghur wheat
1 red chile, seeded and roughly chopped
1 onion, roughly chopped

For the stuffing
1 onion, finely chopped
⅔ cup pine nuts
2 tablespoons olive oil
1½ teaspoons ground allspice
4 tablespoons chopped cilantro

1 If necessary, roughly cut up the lamb and process the pieces in a blender or food processor until minced. Divide the meat into two equal portions.

2 For the patties, soak the bulghur wheat for 15 minutes in cold water. Drain then process in a blender or a food processor with the chile, onion, half the meat and salt and pepper.

3 For the stuffing, fry the onion and pine nuts in the oil for 5 minutes. Add the allspice and remaining meat and fry gently, breaking up the meat with a wooden spoon, until browned. Stir in the cilantro and seasoning.

4 Turn the patty mixture out on to a work surface and shape into a cake. Cut into 12 wedges.

5 Flatten one piece and spoon some stuffing into the center. Bring the edges of the patty up over the stuffing, ensuring that the filling is completely encased.

6 Heat oil to a depth of 2 inches in a large pan until a few patty crumbs sizzle on the surface.

7 Lower half of the filled patties into the oil and fry for about 5 minutes, until golden. Drain on paper towels and keep hot while cooking the remainder. Serve with avocado slices and cilantro sprigs.

Chicken with Lemon and Garlic

Extremely easy to cook and delicious to eat, serve this succulent tapas dish with homemade aïoli, if desired.

INGREDIENTS

Serves 4

8 ounces skinless chicken breast fillets

2 tablespoons olive oil

1 shallot, finely chopped

4 garlic cloves, finely chopped

1 teaspoon paprika

juice of 1 lemon

2 tablespoons chopped fresh parsley

salt and ground black pepper

flat-leaf parsley, to garnish

lemon wedges, to serve

1 Sandwich the chicken breast fillets between two sheets of plastic wrap or waxed paper. Bat with a rolling pin or meat mallet until the fillets are about ¼-inch thick.

2 Cut the chicken into strips about ½ inch wide. Heat the oil in a large frying pan. Stir-fry the chicken strips with the shallot, garlic and paprika over high heat for about 3 minutes, until lightly browned and cooked through. Add the lemon juice and parsley with salt and pepper to taste. Serve with lemon wedges, garnished with flat-leaf parsley.

APPETIZERS FOR
SPECIAL
OCCASIONS

Asparagus with Raspberry Dressing

Asparagus and raspberries complement each other. The sauce gives this appetizer a real zing.

Serves 4

1½ pounds thin asparagus spears

2 tablespoons raspberry vinegar

½ teaspoon salt

1 teaspoon Dijon mustard

1½ tablespoons sunflower oil

2 tablespoons sour cream or plain yogurt

ground white pepper

1 cup fresh raspberries

1 Fill a large wide frying pan or wok with water 4 inches deep and bring to a boil.

2 Trim the tough ends of the asparagus spears. If desired, remove the "scales" using a vegetable peeler.

3 Tie the asparagus spears into two bundles. Lower the bundles into the boiling water and cook until just tender, about 2 minutes.

4 Using a spatula slice, carefully remove the asparagus bundles from the frying pan or wok and immerse in cold water. Drain, then untie the bundles. Pat dry with paper towels. Chill the asparagus in the refrigerator for at least 1 hour.

5 Combine the vinegar and salt in a bowl and stir with a fork until dissolved. Stir in the mustard. Gradually stir in the oil until it is blended. Add the sour cream or yogurt and pepper to taste.

6 To serve, place the asparagus on individual plates and drizzle the dressing on the middle of the spears. Garnish with the fresh raspberries.

Wild Mushroom and Fontina Tarts

Italian fontina cheese gives these tarts a creamy, nutty flavor. Serve them warm with arugula leaves.

INGREDIENTS

Serves 4

½ cup dried wild mushrooms

2 tablespoons olive oil

1 red onion, chopped

2 garlic cloves, chopped

2 tablespoons medium-dry sherry

1 egg

½ cup light cream

1 ounce fontina cheese, thinly sliced

salt and ground black pepper

arugula leaves, to serve

For the pastry

1 cup whole-wheat flour

4 tablespoons unsalted butter

¼ cup walnuts, roasted and ground

1 egg, lightly beaten

1 To make the pastry, rub the flour and butter together until the mixture resembles fine bread crumbs. Add the nuts then the egg; mix into a soft dough. Wrap, then chill for 30 minutes.

2 Meanwhile, soak the dried wild mushrooms in 1¼ cups boiling water for 30 minutes. Drain and reserve the liquid. Fry the onion in the oil for 5 minutes, then add the garlic and fry for about 2 minutes, stirring.

3 Add the soaked mushrooms and cook for 7 minutes over high heat, until the edges become crisp. Add the sherry and the reserved liquid. Cook over high heat for about 10 minutes, until the liquid evaporates. Season and set aside to cool.

COOK'S TIP

You can prepare the pastry shells in advance, bake them blind for 10 minutes, then store in an airtight container for up to 2 days.

---

4 Preheat the oven to 400°F. Lightly grease four 4-inch tart pans. Roll out the pastry on a lightly floured work surface and use to line the tart pans.

5 Prick the pastry, line with waxed paper and baking beans and bake blind for about 10 minutes. Remove the paper and the beans.

6 Whisk the egg and cream to mix, add to the mushroom mixture, then season to taste. Spoon into the pastry shells, top with cheese slices and bake for 18 minutes, until the filling is set. Serve warm with arugula.

Tomato and Zucchini Timbales

Timbales are baked, savory custards typical of the South of France and mainly made with light vegetables. This combination is delicious as an appetizer. It can be served warm or cool. Try other combinations, if desired, and choose different herbs as well.

INGREDIENTS

Serves 4

a little butter

2 zucchini, about 6 ounces

2 firm, ripe vine tomatoes, sliced

2 eggs plus 2 egg yolks

3 tablespoons heavy cream

1 tablespoon fresh tomato sauce or passata

2 teaspoons chopped fresh basil or
    oregano or 1 teaspoon dried

salt and ground black pepper

salad greens, to serve

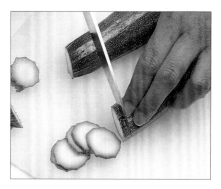

1 Preheat the oven to 350°F. Lightly butter four large ramekins. Trim the zucchini, then cut them into thin slices. Put them into a steamer and steam over boiling water for 4–5 minutes. Drain well in a colander, then layer the zucchini in the ramekins alternating with the sliced tomatoes.

2 Whisk together the eggs, cream, tomato sauce or passata, herbs and seasoning. Pour the egg mixture into the ramekins. Place them in a roasting pan and half fill with hot water. Bake the ramekins for 20–30 minutes, until the custard is just firm.

3 Cool slightly, then run a knife round the rims and carefully turn out onto small plates. Serve with salad greens.

COOK'S TIP

Don't overcook the timbales, or the texture of the savory custard will become rubbery.

Risotto with Four Cheeses

This is a very rich dish. Serve it for a special dinner-party first course, with a light, dry sparkling white wine to accompany it.

INGREDIENTS

Serves 4–6

3 tablespoons butter

1 small onion, finely chopped

5 cups chicken stock,
    preferably homemade

1¾ cups risotto rice

scant 1 cup dry white wine

½ cup grated Gruyère cheese

½ cup diced taleggio cheese

½ cup diced Gorgonzola cheese

⅔ cup freshly grated Parmesan cheese

salt and ground black pepper

chopped fresh flat-leaf parsley, to garnish

1 Melt the butter in a large, heavy saucepan or deep frying pan and fry the onion over low heat for 4–5 minutes, stirring frequently, until softened and lightly browned. Pour the stock into a separate pan and heat it to the simmering point.

2 Add the rice to the onion mixture, stir until the grains start to swell and burst, then add the wine. Stir until it stops sizzling and most of it has been absorbed by the rice, then pour in a little of the hot stock. Add salt and ground black pepper to taste. Stir the rice over low heat until the stock has been absorbed.

3 Gradually add the remaining stock, a little at a time, letting the rice absorb the liquid before adding more, stirring constantly. After 20–25 minutes, the rice will be *al dente* and the risotto will have a creamy consistency.

4 Turn off the heat under the pan, then add the Gruyère, taleggio, the Gorgonzola and 2 tablespoons of the Parmesan. Stir gently until the cheeses have melted, then taste for seasoning. Spoon into a serving bowl and garnish with parsley. Pass the remaining Parmesan separately.

Vegetable Tarte Tatin

This upside-down tart combines Mediterranean vegetables with rice, garlic, onions and olives.

Serves 4

2 tablespoons sunflower oil

about 1½ tablespoons olive oil

1 eggplant, sliced lengthwise

1 large red bell pepper, seeded and cut
    into long strips

5 tomatoes

2 red shallots, finely chopped

1–2 garlic cloves, crushed

⅔ cup white wine

2 teaspoons chopped fresh basil

2 cups cooked white or brown long grain
    rice

⅔ cup pitted black olives, chopped

12 ounces puff pastry, thawed if frozen

ground black pepper

salad greens, to serve

1 Preheat the oven to 375°F. Heat the sunflower oil with 1 tablespoon of the olive oil and fry the eggplant slices for 4–5 minutes on each side. Drain on paper towels.

COOK'S TIP

Zucchini and mushrooms could be used as well, or instead of, the eggplant and bell peppers, or use strips of lightly browned chicken.

---

2 Add the pepper strips to the oil remaining in the pan, turning them to coat. Cover the pan with a lid or aluminum foil and sweat the peppers over medium high heat for 5–6 minutes, stirring occasionally, until the pepper strips are soft and flecked with brown.

3 Slice two of the tomatoes and set them aside. Plunge the remaining tomatoes briefly into boiling water, then peel them, cut them into quarters and remove the core and seeds. Chop the tomato flesh roughly.

4 Heat the remaining oil in the frying pan and fry the shallots and garlic for 3–4 minutes, until softened. Then add the chopped tomatoes and cook for a few minutes, until softened. Stir in the wine and basil, with black pepper to taste. Bring to a boil, then remove from the heat and stir in the cooked rice and black olives.

5 Arrange the tomato slices, eggplant slices and peppers in a single layer on the bottom of a heavy, 12-inch, shallow ovenproof dish. Spread the rice mixture on top.

6 Roll out the pastry to a circle slightly larger than the diameter of the dish and place on top of the rice, tucking the overlap down inside the dish.

7 Bake for 25–30 minutes, until the pastry is golden and risen. Cool slightly, then invert the tart onto a large, warmed serving plate. Serve in slices, with some salad greens.

Black Pasta with Ricotta

This is designer pasta—colored with squid ink—at its most dramatic, the kind of dish you are most likely to see at a fashionable Italian restaurant. Serve it for a stylish dinner-party first course—it will be a great centerpiece.

INGREDIENTS

Serves 4

11 ounces dried black pasta

4 tablespoons ricotta cheese, as fresh as possible

4 tablespoons extra virgin olive oil

1 small fresh red chile, seeded and finely chopped

small handful of fresh basil leaves

salt and ground black pepper

1 Cook the black pasta in salted boiling water according to the instructions on the package. Meanwhile, put the ricotta in a bowl, add salt and pepper to taste and use a little of the hot water from the pasta pan to mix it into a smooth, creamy consistency. Taste for seasoning.

2 Drain the pasta. Heat the oil gently in the clean pan and add the pasta with the chile and salt and pepper to taste. Toss quickly over high heat to combine.

3 Divide the pasta equally among four warmed bowls, then top with the ricotta cheese. Sprinkle with the basil leaves and serve immediately. Each diner tosses their own portion of pasta and cheese.

COOK'S TIP

If you prefer, use green spinach-flavored pasta or red tomato-flavored pasta instead of the black pasta.

Paglia e Fieno with Walnuts and Gorgonzola

Cheese and nuts are popular ingredients for pasta sauces. The combination is very rich, so reserve this dish for a dinner-party appetizer. The contrasting colors make this dish look particularly attractive. It needs no accompaniment other than wine—a dry white would be good.

INGREDIENTS

Serves 4

10 ounces dried paglia e fieno

2 tablespoons butter

1 teaspoon finely chopped fresh sage, or ½ teaspoon dried, plus fresh sage leaves, to garnish (optional)

1 cup Gorgonzola cheese, diced

3 tablespoons mascarpone cheese

5 tablespoons milk

½ cup walnut halves, ground

2 tablespoons freshly grated Parmesan cheese

ground black pepper

1 Cook the pasta in a large saucepan of salted boiling water, according to the instructions on the package. Meanwhile, melt the butter in a large skillet or saucepan over low heat, add the sage and stir it around. Sprinkle in the diced Gorgonzola and then add the mascarpone. Stir the ingredients with a wooden spoon until the cheeses start to melt. Pour in the milk and keep stirring.

2 Sprinkle in the walnuts and grated Parmesan and add plenty of black pepper. Continue to stir over low heat until the mixture forms a creamy sauce. Do not let it boil or the nuts will taste bitter, and do not cook the sauce for longer than a few minutes or the nuts will begin to discolor it.

3 Drain the pasta, put it into a warmed bowl, then add the sauce and toss well. Serve immediately, with more black pepper ground on top. Garnish with sage leaves, if using.

Lemon, Thyme and Bean Stuffed Mushrooms

Portabello mushrooms have a rich flavor and a meaty texture that go well with this fragrant herb-and-lemon stuffing. The garlicky pine nut accompaniment is a traditional Middle Eastern dish with a smooth, creamy consistency similar to that of hummus.

INGREDIENTS

Serves 4–6

1 cup dried or 2 cups drained, canned
    adzuki beans
3 tablespoons olive oil, plus extra
    for brushing
1 onion, finely chopped
2 garlic cloves, crushed
2 tablespoons fresh chopped thyme or
    1 teaspoon dried
8 large field mushrooms, such as
    portabello mushrooms, stalks
    finely chopped
1 cup fresh whole-wheat bread crumbs
juice of 1 lemon
¾ cup goat cheese, crumbled
salt and ground black pepper

For the pine nut sauce
½ cup pine nuts, toasted
1 cup cubed white bread
2 garlic cloves, chopped
scant 1 cup milk
3 tablespoons olive oil
1 tablespoon chopped fresh parsley, to
    garnish (optional)

1 If using dried beans, soak them overnight, then drain and rinse well. Place in a saucepan, add enough water to cover and bring to a boil. Boil rapidly for 10 minutes, then reduce the heat, cook for 30 minutes, until tender, and drain. If using canned beans, rinse, drain well, then set aside.

2 Preheat the oven to 400°F. Heat the oil in a large heavy frying pan, add the onion and garlic and sauté for 5 minutes, until softened. Add the thyme and the mushroom stalks and cook for another 3 minutes, stirring occasionally, until tender.

3 Stir in the beans, bread crumbs and lemon juice, season well, then cook for 2 minutes, until heated through. Mash two-thirds of the beans with a fork or potato masher, leaving the remaining beans whole.

4 Brush a baking dish and the bottom and sides of the mushrooms with oil, then top each one with a spoonful of the bean mixture. Place the mushrooms in the dish, cover with aluminum foil and bake for 20 minutes. Remove the foil. Top each mushroom with some of the goat cheese and bake for another 15 minutes or until the cheese is melted and bubbly and the mushrooms are tender.

5 To make the pine nut sauce, place all the ingredients in a food processor or blender and blend until smooth and creamy. Add more milk if the mixture appears too thick. Sprinkle with parsley, if using, and serve with the stuffed mushrooms.

Eggplant and Smoked Mozzarella Rolls

Slices of broiled eggplant are stuffed with smoked mozzarella, tomato and fresh basil to make an attractive hors-d'oeuvre. The rolls are also good grilled.

INGREDIENTS

Serves 4

1 large eggplant

3 tablespoons olive oil, plus extra for drizzling (optional)

5½ ounces smoked mozzarella cheese, cut into 8 slices

2 plum tomatoes, each cut into 4 even-size slices

8 large basil leaves

balsamic vinegar, for drizzling (optional)

salt and ground black pepper

1 Cut the eggplant lengthwise into 10 thin slices and discard the two outermost slices. Sprinkle the slices with salt and set them aside for 20 minutes. Rinse, then pat dry with paper towels.

2 Preheat the broiler and line a broiler pan with aluminum foil. Place the dried eggplant slices on the broiler pan and brush liberally with oil. Broil for 8–10 minutes, until tender and golden, turning once.

3 Remove the eggplant slices from the broiler, then place a slice of mozzarella and tomato and a basil leaf in the center of each eggplant slice, and season to taste. Fold the eggplant over the filling and cook seam-side down under the broiler until heated through and the mozzarella begins to melt. Serve drizzled with olive oil and a little balsamic vinegar, if using.

Smoked Salmon and Rice Salad Parcels

Feta, cucumber and tomatoes give a Greek flavor to the salad in these parcels, a combination that goes well with the rice, especially if a little wild rice is added.

INGREDIENTS

Serves 4

scant 1 cup mixed wild rice and
    basmati rice
8 slices smoked salmon, total weight
    about 12 ounces
4-inch piece of cucumber, finely diced
about 8 ounces feta cheese, cubed
8 cherry tomatoes, quartered
2 tablespoons mayonnaise
2 teaspoons fresh lime juice
1 tablespoon chopped fresh chervil
salt and ground black pepper
lime slices and fresh chervil, to garnish

1 Cook the rice according to the instructions on the package. Drain, put in a bowl and let cool completely.

2 Line four ramekins with plastic wrap, then line each ramekin with two slices of smoked salmon, letting the ends overlap the edges of the dishes.

COOK'S TIP

Use smoked trout instead of the salmon, if desired.

---

3 Add the cucumber, feta and tomatoes to the rice, and stir in the mayonnaise, lime juice and chervil. Combine well. Season with salt and ground black pepper to taste.

4 Spoon the rice mixture into the salmon-lined ramekins. (Any leftover mixture can be used to make a rice salad.) Then fold over the overlapping ends of salmon so that the rice mixture is completely encased.

5 Chill the parcels in the refrigerator for 30–60 minutes, then invert each parcel onto a plate, using the plastic wrap to ease them out of the ramekins. Carefully peel off the plastic wrap, then garnish each parcel with slices of lime and a sprig of fresh chervil and serve.

Quail's Eggs in Aspic with Prosciutto

These unusual-looking eggs in aspic are so easy to make and are great for summer eating. Serve them with salad greens and some homemade mayonnaise on the side.

INGREDIENTS

Makes 12

1 envelope aspic or unflavored gelatin

3 tablespoons dry sherry

12 quail's eggs

6 slices of prosciutto

12 fresh cilantro or flat-leaf parsley leaves

salad greens, to serve

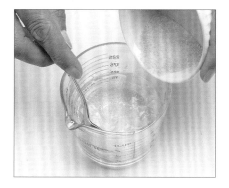

1 Make the aspic following the package instructions but replace 3 tablespoons water with the dry sherry, giving a greater depth of flavor. Leave the aspic in the refrigerator until it begins to thicken, but not too much.

2 Put the quail's eggs in a pan of cold water and bring to a boil. Boil for 1½ minutes, then pour off the hot water and leave in cold water until cold. This way the yolks should still be a little soft, but the whites will be firm enough to peel when really cold.

3 Rinse 12 dariole molds so they are damp and place them on a tray. Cut the prosciutto into 12 pieces, then roll or fold so they will fit into the molds.

4 Place an herb leaf in the bottom of each mold, then put a peeled egg on top. As the aspic begins to thicken, pour in enough to nearly cover each egg, holding it steady. Then put the slice of prosciutto on the egg and pour in the rest of the aspic to fill the mold, so that when you turn them out the eggs will be sitting on the prosciutto.

5 Transfer the tray of molds to a cold place for 3–4 hours, until set and cold. When ready to serve, run a knife around the top rim to loosen. Dip the molds into warm, not hot, water and shake or tap gently until they appear loose. Invert onto small plates and serve with salad greens.

Egg and Salmon Parcels

These crisp elegant parcels hide a mouthwatering collection of flavors and textures. and make a delicious appetizer or lunch dish.

INGREDIENTS

Serves 6

scant ½ cup long grain rice

1¼ cups fish stock

12 ounces piece salmon tail

juice of ½ lemon

1 tablespoon chopped fresh dill

1 tablespoon chopped fresh parsley

2 teaspoons mild curry powder

6 small eggs, soft-boiled and cooled

15 ounces puff pastry, thawed if frozen

1 small egg, beaten

salt and ground black pepper

1 Cook the rice in the fish stock according to the package instructions, then drain and set aside to cool. Preheat the oven to 425°F.

2 Poach the salmon, then remove the bones and skin and flake the fish into the rice. Add the lemon juice, herbs, curry powder and seasoning and mix well. Peel the eggs.

COOK'S TIP

～

You can also add a spoonful of cooked chopped fresh or frozen spinach to each parcel.

3 Roll out the pastry and cut into six 5½–6-inch squares. Brush the edges with the beaten egg. Place a spoonful of rice in the middle of each square, push an egg into the middle and top with a little more rice.

4 Pull over the pastry corners to the middle to form a square parcel, squeezing the seams together well to seal. Brush with more egg, place on a baking sheet and bake the puffs for 20 minutes, then reduce the oven temperature to 375°F and cook the puffs for another 10 minutes or until golden and crisp underneath.

5 Cool slightly before serving, with a curry flavored mayonnaise or Hollandaise sauce, if desired.

Hot Crab Soufflés

These delicious little soufflés must be served as soon as they are ready, so seat your guests at the table before taking the soufflés out of the oven.

INGREDIENTS

Serves 6

¼ cup butter

3 tablespoons fine whole-wheat
   bread crumbs

4 scallions, finely chopped

1 tablespoon Malayan or mild Madras
   curry powder

2 tablespoons all-purpose flour

7 tablespoons coconut milk or milk

⅔ cup whipping cream

4 egg yolks

8 ounces white crab meat

mild green Tabasco sauce

6 egg whites

salt and ground black pepper

1 Use some of the butter to grease six ramekin dishes or a 7½-cup soufflé dish. Sprinkle in the fine whole-wheat bread crumbs, roll the dishes or dish around to coat the bottom and sides completely, then pour out the excess bread crumbs. Preheat the oven to 400°F.

2 Melt the remaining butter in a saucepan, add the scallions and Malayan or mild Madras curry powder and cook over low heat for about 1 minute, until softened. Stir in the flour and cook for another minute.

3 Gradually add the coconut milk or milk and the cream, stirring constantly. Cook until smooth and thick. Off the heat, stir in the egg yolks, then the crab. Season with salt, black pepper and Tabasco sauce.

4 In a grease-free bowl, beat the egg whites stiffly with a pinch of salt. With a metal spoon, stir one-third into the crab mixture then fold in the rest. Spoon into the dishes or dish.

5 Bake until well risen, golden brown and just firm to the touch. Individual soufflés will take 8 minutes; a large soufflé will take 15–20 minutes. Serve immediately.

S
The
smo
wor

Serv
For
1 cu
pinc
1 eg
1¼
1 tal
    fo
2–3
frisé

For
8 ou
8 ou
1¼
⅔ c
3 tal
¼ c
fresl
2 ha
salt

1
Ma
the
egg
of t

2
bat
cor
the

Tiger Shrimp with Mint, Dill and Lime

A wonderful combination—mint, dill and lime blend together to make a magical concoction to flavor succulent tiger shrimp that will delight everyone who tries it.

INGREDIENTS

Serves 4

4 large sheets phyllo pastry

⅓ cup butter

16 large tiger shrimp, cooked and peeled

1 tablespoon chopped fresh mint, plus
    extra to garnish

1 tablespoon chopped fresh dill

juice of 1 lime

8 cooked unpeeled tiger shrimp and
    lime wedges, to serve

1 Keep the sheets of phyllo pastry covered with a dry, clean cloth to keep them moist. Cut one sheet of phyllo pastry in half widthwise and brush with melted butter. Place one half on top of the other.

2 Preheat the oven to 450°F. Cut the tiger shrimp in half down the back of the shrimp and remove the dark vein.

3 Place four shrimp in the center of the phyllo pastry and sprinkle a quarter of the mint, dill and lime juice on top. Fold over the sides, brush with butter and roll up to make a parcel.

4 Once you have filled all the parcels, place them seam side down, on a greased baking sheet. Bake for 10 minutes or until golden. Serve with whole tiger shrimp, lime wedges and mint.

Scallop-stuffed Roast Bell Peppers with Pesto

Serve these scallop-and-pesto-filled sweet red bell peppers with Italian bread, such as ciabatta or focaccia, to mop up the garlicky juices.

INGREDIENTS

Serves 4

4 squat red bell peppers

2 large garlic cloves, cut into thin slivers

4 tablespoons olive oil

4 shelled scallops

3 tablespoons pesto

salt and ground black pepper

freshly grated Parmesan cheese, to serve

salad greens and basil sprigs, to garnish

1 Preheat the oven to 350°F. Cut the peppers in half lengthwise, through their stalks. Scrape out and discard the cores and seeds. Wash the pepper shells and pat dry with paper towels.

2 Put the peppers, cut-side up, in an oiled roasting pan. Divide the slivers of garlic equally among them and sprinkle with salt and ground black pepper to taste. Then spoon the oil into the peppers and roast for 40 minutes.

3 Using a sharp knife, carefully cut each of the shelled scallops in half horizontally to make two flat discs each with a piece of coral. When cooked, remove the peppers from the oven and place a scallop half in each pepper half. Then top with the pesto.

4 Return the pan to the oven and roast for 10 more minutes. Transfer the peppers to individual serving plates, sprinkle with grated Parmesan and garnish each plate with a few salad greens and basil sprigs. Serve warm.

COOK'S TIP

Scallops are available at most fishmongers and supermarkets with fresh fish counters. Never cook scallops for longer than the time stated in the recipe, or they will be tough and rubbery.

Jumbo Shrimp in Sherry

This dish just couldn't be simpler. The sherry brings out the sweetness of the seafood perfectly.

INGREDIENTS

Serves 4

12 jumbo shrimp, peeled

2 tablespoons olive oil

2 tablespoons sherry

few drops of Tabasco sauce

salt and ground black pepper

1 Using a very sharp knife, make a shallow cut down the back of each shrimp, then pull out and discard the dark intestinal tract.

2 Heat the oil in a frying pan and fry the shrimp for 2–3 minutes, until pink. Pour on the sherry and season with Tabasco sauce and salt and pepper. Turn into a dish and serve the shrimp immediately.

Sizzling Shrimp

This dish works especially well with tiny shrimp that can be eaten whole, but any type of unpeeled shrimp will be fine. Choose a small casserole or frying pan that can be taken to the table for serving while the garlicky shrimp are still sizzling and piping hot.

INGREDIENTS

Serves 4

2 garlic cloves, halved

2 tablespoons butter

1 small red chile, seeded and finely sliced

1 cup unpeeled cooked shrimp

sea salt and coarsely ground black pepper

lime wedges, to serve

1 Rub the cut surfaces of the garlic cloves on the bottom and sides of a frying pan, then throw the garlic cloves away. Add the butter to the pan and melt over fairly high heat until it just begins to turn golden brown.

2 Toss in the sliced red chile and the shrimp. Stir-fry for 1–2 minutes, until heated through, then season to taste with sea salt and plenty of black pepper. Serve directly from the pan with lime wedges for squeezing on top.

COOK'S TIP

Wear gloves when handling chiles, or wash your hands thoroughly afterward, as the juices can cause severe irritation to sensitive skin, especially around the eyes, nose or mouth.

Garlic Shrimp in Phyllo Tartlets

Tartlets made with crisp layers of phyllo pastry and filled with garlic shrimp make a tempting dish.

INGREDIENTS

Serves 4

For the tartlets

4 tablespoons butter, melted

2–3 large sheets phyllo pastry

For the filling

½ cup butter

2–3 garlic cloves, crushed

1 red chile, seeded and chopped

3 cups cooked peeled shrimp

2 tablespoons chopped fresh parsley or
   snipped fresh chives

salt and ground black pepper

1 Preheat the oven to 400°F. Brush four individual 3-inch flan pans with melted butter.

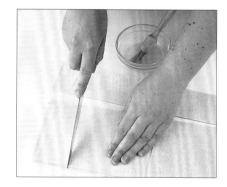

2 Cut the phyllo pastry into twelve 4-inch squares and brush with the melted butter.

3 Place three squares inside each pan, overlapping them at slight angles and carefully frilling the edges and points while forming a good hollow in each center. Bake for 10–15 minutes, until crisp and golden. Let cool slightly then remove the pastry shells from the pans.

4 Meanwhile, make the filling. Melt the butter in a large frying pan, then add the garlic, chile and shrimp and fry quickly for 1–2 minutes to warm through. Stir in the fresh parsley or chives and season with salt and plenty of black pepper.

5 Spoon the shrimp filling into the tartlets and serve immediately, perhaps with some sour cream.

Clams with Chili and Yellow Bean Sauce

This delicious Thai-inspired dish is simple to prepare. It can be made in a matter of minutes so will not keep you away from your guests for very long.

INGREDIENTS

Serves 4–6

2¼ pounds fresh clams

2 tablespoons vegetable oil

4 garlic cloves, finely chopped

1 tablespoon grated fresh ginger

4 shallots, finely chopped

2 tablespoons yellow bean sauce

6 red chiles, seeded and chopped

1 tablespoon fish sauce

pinch of sugar

handful of basil leaves, plus extra
   to garnish

1 Wash and scrub the clams. Heat the oil in a wok or large frying pan. Add the garlic and ginger and fry for 30 seconds, add the shallots and fry for another minute.

2 Add the clams to the pan. Using a spatula, turn them a few times to coat all over with the oil. Add the yellow bean sauce and half the chopped red chiles.

3 Continue to cook, stirring often, for 5–7 minutes, or until all the clams open. You may need to add a splash of water. Adjust the seasoning with the fish sauce and a little sugar.

4 Finally add the basil leaves and stir to mix. Transfer the clams to individual bowls or a serving platter. Garnish with the remaining red chiles and basil leaves. Serve immediately.

Crab Cakes with Tartar Sauce

Sweet crab meat is offset by a piquant tartar sauce.

Serves 4

1½ pounds fresh lump crab meat

1 egg, beaten

2 tablespoons mayonnaise

1 tablespoon Worcestershire sauce

1 tablespoon sherry

2 tablespoons minced fresh parsley

1 tablespoon minced fresh chives or dill

salt and ground black pepper

3 tablespoons olive oil

salad greens, chives and lemon, to garnish

For the sauce

1 egg yolk

1 tablespoon white wine vinegar

2 tablespoons Dijon-style mustard

1 cup vegetable or peanut oil

2 tablespoons fresh lemon juice

4 tablespoons minced scallions

2 tablespoons chopped drained capers

4 tablespoons minced dill pickles

4 tablespoons minced fresh parsley

1 Pick through the crab meat, removing any pieces of shell or cartilage. Keep the pieces of crab as large as possible.

2 In a mixing bowl, combine the beaten egg with the mayonnaise, Worcestershire sauce, sherry and herbs. Season with salt and lots of black pepper. Gently fold in the crab meat.

3 Divide the mixture into 8 portions and gently form each one into an oval cake. Place on a baking sheet between layers of waxed paper and chill for at least 1 hour.

4 Meanwhile, make the sauce. In a medium-size bowl, beat the egg yolk with a wire whisk until smooth. Add the vinegar, mustard, and salt and pepper to taste, and whisk for about 10 seconds to blend. Slowly whisk in the oil.

5 Add the lemon juice, scallions, capers, pickles and parsley, and mix well. Check the seasoning. Cover and chill.

6 Preheat the broiler. Brush the crab cakes with the olive oil. Place on an oiled baking sheet, in one layer.

7 Broil 6 inches from the heat until golden brown, about 5 minutes on each side. Serve the crab cakes with the tartar sauce, garnished with salad greens, chives and lemon.

COOK'S TIP

For easier handling and to make the crab meat go further, add 1 cup fresh bread crumbs and 1 more egg to the crab mixture. Divide the mixture into 12 cakes to serve 6.

Scallops Wrapped in Prosciutto

*Cook these skewers on the grill for
al fresco summer dining. Serve with
lime wedges for a sharper flavor.*

INGREDIENTS

Serves 4

24 shucked medium-size scallops,
    corals removed
lemon juice
8–12 prosciutto slices, cut lengthwise into
    2 or 3 strips
olive oil, for brushing
ground black pepper
lemon wedges, to serve

1 Prepare the grill well in
advance or preheat the broiler
when you make the skewers.

2 Sprinkle the scallops with
lemon juice. Wrap a strip of
prosciutto around each scallop.
Thread onto 8 skewers.

3 Brush with oil. Arrange on a
baking sheet if broiling. Broil
about 4 inches from the heat, or
cook over the grill, for 3–5 minutes
on each side or until the scallops
are opaque.

4 Set 2 skewers on each plate.
Sprinkle the scallops with
freshly ground black pepper and
serve with lemon wedges.

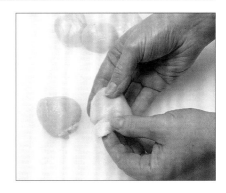

COOK'S TIP

Use a short sturdy knife to pry
shelled scallops open. Discard the
membrane, organs and gristle at
the side of the white meat. Set the
coral aside. Rinse well.

Mussels and Clams with Lemongrass

Lemongrass has an incomparable flavor and is excellent used with seafood. If you cannot find clams, use extra mussels instead.

INGREDIENTS

Serves 6

4–4½ pounds mussels

1 pound baby clams, washed

½ cup dry white wine

1 bunch scallions, chopped

2 lemongrass stalks, chopped

6 kaffir lime leaves, chopped

2 teaspoons Thai green curry paste

scant 1 cup coconut cream

2 tablespoons chopped fresh cilantro

salt and ground black pepper

whole garlic chives, to garnish

1 Clean the mussels. Pull off the beards and scrub the shells. Discard any that are broken or stay open when tapped.

2 Put the wine, scallions, lemongrass, lime leaves and curry paste in a pan. Simmer until the wine almost evaporates.

3 Add the mussels and clams to the pan, cover tightly and steam the shellfish over high heat for 5–6 minutes, until they open.

4 Using a slotted spoon, transfer the mussels and clams to a warmed serving bowl and keep hot. Discard any shellfish that remain closed. Strain the cooking liquid into a clean saucepan and then simmer to reduce the amount to about 1 cup.

5 Stir in the coconut cream and cilantro, with salt and pepper to taste. Heat through. Pour onto the seafood and serve, garnished with garlic chives.

COOK'S TIP
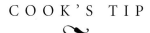

Buy a few extra mussels just in case there are any that have to be discarded.

Shrimp Cocktail

There is no nicer appetizer than a good, fresh shrimp cocktail—and nothing worse than one in which soggy shrimp swim in a thin, vinegary sauce embedded in limp lettuce. This recipe shows just how good a shrimp cocktail can be.

INGREDIENTS

Serves 6

4 tablespoons heavy cream, lightly whipped

4 tablespoons mayonnaise,
    preferably homemade

4 tablespoons ketchup

1–2 teaspoons Worcestershire sauce

juice of 1 lemon

½ Romaine lettuce or other
    very crisp lettuce

4 cups cooked peeled shrimp

salt, ground black pepper and paprika

6 large whole cooked unpeeled shrimp,
    to garnish (optional)

thinly sliced brown bread and lemon
    wedges, to serve

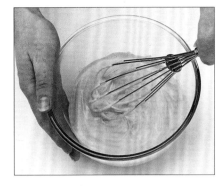

1 In a bowl, combine the whipped cream, mayonnaise and ketchup. Add Worcestershire sauce to taste. Stir in enough lemon juice to make a really tangy cocktail sauce.

2 Finely shred the lettuce and fill six individual glasses one-third full. Stir the shrimp into the sauce, then check the seasoning. Spoon the shrimp mixture generously onto the lettuce.

3 If desired, drape a whole cooked shrimp over the edge of each glass (see Cook's Tip). Sprinkle each of the cocktails with ground black pepper and some paprika. Serve immediately, with thinly sliced brown bread and butter and lemon wedges for squeezing on top.

COOK'S TIP
❧

To prepare the garnish, peel the shell from the shrimp and leave the tail "fan" for decoration.

Aromatic Tiger Shrimp

There is no elegant way to eat these aromatic shrimp—just hold them by the tails, pull them off the sticks with your fingers and pop them into your mouth.

INGREDIENTS

Serves 4

16 raw tiger shrimp or scampi tails

½ teaspoon chili powder

1 teaspoon fennel seeds

5 Szechuan or black peppercorns

1 star anise, broken into segments

1 cinnamon stick, broken into pieces

2 tablespoons peanut or sunflower oil

2 garlic cloves, chopped

¾-inch piece fresh ginger, peeled and
    finely chopped

1 shallot, chopped

2 tablespoons water

2 tablespoons rice vinegar

2 tablespoons brown sugar

salt and ground black pepper

lime slices and chopped scallion,
    to garnish

1 Thread the shrimp or scampi tails in pairs on 8 wooden cocktail sticks. Set aside. Heat a frying pan, put in all the chili powder, fennel seeds, Szechuan or black peppercorns, star anise and cinnamon stick and dry-fry for 1–2 minutes to release the flavors. Let cool, then grind coarsely in a grinder or put in a mortar and crush with a pestle.

2 Heat the peanut or sunflower oil in a shallow pan, add the garlic, ginger and chopped shallot and then fry gently until very lightly colored. Add the crushed spices and seasoning and cook the mixture gently for 2 minutes. Pour in the water and simmer, stirring, for 5 minutes.

3 Add the rice vinegar and brown sugar, stir until dissolved, then add the shrimp or scampi tails. Cook for 3–5 minutes, until the seafood has turned pink but is still very juicy. Serve hot, garnished with lime slices and scallions.

COOK'S TIP

If you buy whole shrimp, remove the heads before cooking them.

Salmon and Scallop Brochettes

With their delicate colors and really superb flavor, these skewers make a perfect opener for a sophisticated dinner party.

INGREDIENTS

Serves 4

8 lemongrass stalks

8 ounces salmon fillet, skinned

8 shucked queen scallops, with their corals if possible

8 baby onions, peeled and blanched

½ yellow bell pepper, cut into 8 squares

2 tablespoons butter

juice of ½ lemon

salt, ground white pepper and paprika

For the sauce

2 tablespoons dry vermouth

¼ cup butter

1 teaspoon chopped fresh tarragon

1 Preheat the broiler to medium-high. Cut off the top 3–4 inches of each lemongrass stalk. Reserve the bulb ends for another dish. Cut the salmon fillet into twelve ¾-inch cubes. Thread the salmon, scallops, corals if available, onions and pepper squares onto the lemongrass and arrange the brochettes in a broiler pan.

2 Melt the butter in a small pan, add the lemon juice and a pinch of paprika and then brush onto the brochettes. Broil the skewers for 2–3 minutes on each side, turning and basting the brochettes every minute, until the fish and scallops are just cooked, but are still very juicy. Transfer to a platter and keep hot while you make the tarragon butter sauce.

3 Pour the dry vermouth and the leftover cooking juices from the brochettes into a small pan and boil fiercely to reduce by half. Add the butter and melt, then stir in the chopped fresh tarragon and salt and ground white pepper to taste. Pour the tarragon butter sauce onto the brochettes and serve.

Marinated Asparagus and Langoustines

For a really extravagant treat, you could make this attractive salad with medallions of lobster. For a cheaper version, use large shrimp, allowing six per serving.

INGREDIENTS

Serves 4

16 langoustines

16 fresh asparagus spears, trimmed

2 carrots

2 tablespoons olive oil

1 garlic clove, peeled

salt and ground black pepper

4 fresh tarragon sprigs and some chopped,
    to garnish

For the dressing

2 tablespoons tarragon vinegar

½ cup olive oil

1 Peel the langoustines and keep the discarded parts for stock. Set aside.

2 Steam the asparagus over boiling salted water until just tender but still a little crisp. Refresh under cold water, drain and place in a shallow dish.

3 Peel the carrots and cut into fine julienne shreds. Cook in a pan of lightly salted boiling water for about 3 minutes, until tender but still crunchy. Drain, refresh under cold water, drain again. Add to the asparagus.

4 Make the dressing. In a pitcher, whisk the tarragon vinegar with the oil. Season to taste. Pour over the asparagus and carrots and let marinate.

5 Heat the oil with the garlic in a frying pan until very hot. Add the langoustines and sauté quickly until just heated through. Discard the garlic.

6 Arrange four asparagus spears and the carrots on four individual plates. Drizzle on the dressing left in the dish and top each portion with four langoustine tails. Top with the tarragon sprigs and sprinkle the chopped tarragon on top. Serve immediately.

COOK'S TIP

Most of the langoustines we buy have been cooked at sea, a necessary act because the flesh deteriorates rapidly after death. Bear this in mind when you cook the shellfish. Because it has already been cooked, it will only need to be lightly sautéed until heated through. If you are lucky enough to buy live langoustines, kill them quickly by immersing them in boiling water, then sauté until cooked through.

Broiled Scallops with Brown Butter

This is a very striking dish, as the scallops are served on the half shell, still sizzling from the broiler. Reserve it for a very special occasion.

INGREDIENTS

Serves 4

¼ cup unsalted butter, diced

8 scallops, prepared on the half shell

1 tablespoon chopped fresh parsley

salt and ground black pepper

lemon wedges, to serve

COOK'S TIP

If you can't get hold of scallops in their shells, you can use shelled, fresh scallops if you cook them on the day of purchase.

1 Preheat the broiler to high. Melt the butter in a small saucepan over medium heat until it is pale golden brown. Remove the pan from the heat immediately; the butter must not burn. Arrange the scallop shells in a single layer in a casserole or a shallow roasting pan. Brush a little of the brown butter onto the scallops.

2 Broil the scallops for 4 minutes —it will not be necessary to turn them. Pour on the remaining brown butter, then sprinkle on a little salt and pepper and parsley. Serve immediately, with lemon wedges for squeezing over.

Fried Squid

The squid is simply dusted in flour and dipped in egg before being fried, so the coating is light and does not mask the flavor.

INGREDIENTS

Serves 2

4 ounces prepared squid, cut into rings

2 tablespoons seasoned all-purpose flour

1 egg

2 tablespoons milk

olive oil, for frying

sea salt, to taste

lemon wedges, to serve

COOK'S TIP

For a crisper coating, dust the rings in flour, then dip them in batter instead of this simple egg and flour coating.

1 Toss the squid rings in the seasoned flour in a bowl or strong plastic bag. Beat the egg and milk together in a shallow bowl. Heat the oil in a heavy-based frying pan.

2 Dip the floured squid rings one at a time into the egg mixture, shaking off any excess liquid. Add to the hot oil, in batches if necessary, and fry for 2–3 minutes on each side until evenly golden all over.

3 Drain the fried squid on paper towels, then sprinkle with salt. Transfer to a small warm plate and serve with the lemon wedges.

Scallop and Mussel Kebabs

These delightfully crispy seafood skewers are served with hot toast spread with fresh herb butter.

INGREDIENTS

Serves 4

5 tablespoons butter, at room temperature

2 tablespoons minced fresh fennel
   or parsley

1 tablespoon lemon juice

32 small scallops

24 large mussels, in the shell

8 strips bacon

1 cup fresh bread crumbs

¼ cup olive oil

salt and ground black pepper

hot toast, to serve

1 Make the flavored butter by combining the butter with the minced herbs and lemon juice. Add salt and pepper to taste. Mix well and set aside.

2 In a small saucepan, cook the scallops in their own liquor until they begin to shrink. (If there is no scallop liquor—retained from the shells after shucking—use a little fish stock or white wine.) Drain the scallops well and then pat dry with paper towels.

3 Scrub the mussels well and remove their beards, then rinse under cold running water. Place in a large saucepan with about 1 inch of water in the bottom. Cover and steam the mussels over medium heat until they open. When cool enough to handle, remove them from their shells, and pat dry using paper towels. Discard any mussels that have not opened during cooking.

4 Take 6-inch wooden or metal skewers. Thread on each one, alternately, 4 scallops and 3 mussels. As you are doing this, weave a strip of bacon between the scallops and mussels.

5 Preheat the broiler. Spread the bread crumbs on a plate. Brush the seafood with olive oil and roll in the crumbs to coat all over.

6 Place the skewers on the broiler pan. Broil until crisp and lightly browned, 4–5 minutes on each side. Serve immediately with hot toast and the flavored butter.

Monkfish Packages

Notoriously ugly, the monkfish makes delicious eating with its faintly shellfish-like flavor. You could use a cheaper fish, but you'll lose that taste.

INGREDIENTS

Serves 4

1½ cups bread flour

2 eggs

4 ounces skinless monkfish fillet, diced

grated zest of 1 lemon

1 garlic clove, chopped

1 small red chile, seeded and sliced

3 tablespoons chopped fresh parsley

2 tablespoons light cream

salt and ground black pepper

For the tomato oil

2 tomatoes, peeled, seeded and
    finely diced

3 tablespoons extra virgin olive oil

1 tablespoon lemon juice

1 Place the bread flour, eggs and ½ teaspoon salt in a blender or food processor; pulse until it forms a soft dough. Knead for 2–3 minutes. Wrap in plastic wrap and chill for 20 minutes.

2 Place the monkfish, lemon zest, garlic, chile and parsley in the clean food processor; process until very finely chopped. Add the cream, with plenty of salt and ground black pepper, and process again until a very thick paste is formed.

3 Make the tomato oil by stirring the diced tomatoes with the olive oil and lemon juice in a bowl. Add salt to taste. Cover and chill.

COOK'S TIP

If the dough is sticky, sprinkle a little flour into the bowl of the food processor.

4 Roll out the dough thinly on a lightly floured surface and cut out 32 rounds, using a 1½-inch plain cutter. Divide the filling among half the rounds, then cover with the remaining rounds. Pinch the edges tightly to seal, trying to exclude as much air as possible.

5 Bring a large saucepan of water to a simmer and poach the fish packages in batches, for 2–3 minutes or until they rise to the surface. Drain and serve hot, drizzled with the tomato oil.

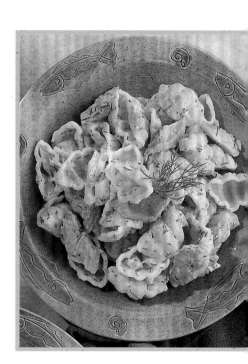

SALADS

Pear and Parmesan Salad

This is a good dish when pears are at their seasonal best. Try Packhams or Comice when plentiful, drizzled with a poppy-seed dressing and topped with shavings of Parmesan.

INGREDIENTS

Serves 4

4 just-ripe dessert pears

2-ounce piece Parmesan cheese

watercress, to garnish

water crackers or rye bread,
    to serve (optional)

For the dressing

2 tablespoons extra virgin olive oil

1 tablespoon sunflower oil

2 tablespoons cider vinegar or white
    wine vinegar

½ teaspoon light brown sugar

good pinch of dried thyme

1 tablespoon poppy seeds

salt and ground black pepper

1 Cut the pears in quarters and remove the cores. Cut each pear quarter in half lengthwise and arrange them on four small serving plates. Peel the pears if desired, though they look more attractive unpeeled.

2 Make the dressing. Mix the oils, vinegar, sugar, thyme and seasoning in a pitcher. Whisk well, then add the poppy seeds. Trickle the dressing onto the pears. Garnish with watercress and shave Parmesan on top. Serve with water crackers or thinly sliced rye bread, if desired.

COOK'S TIP

Blue cheeses and pears also have a natural affinity. Stilton, dolcelatte, Gorgonzola or Danish blue are good substitutes. Allow about 7 ounces and cut into wedges or cubes. This makes a slightly more substantial first course, so follow with a light dish.

Panzanella Salad

If sliced juicy tomatoes layered with day-old bread sounds strange for a salad, don't be deceived —it's quite delicious. A popular Italian salad, this dish is ideal for serving as an appetizer. Use full-flavored tomatoes for the best results.

INGREDIENTS

Serves 4–6

4 thick slices day-old bread, either white, brown or rye

1 small red onion, thinly sliced

1 pound ripe tomatoes, thinly sliced

4 ounces mozzarella cheese, thinly sliced

1 tablespoon fresh basil, shredded, or fresh marjoram

½ cup extra virgin olive oil

3 tablespoons balsamic vinegar

juice or 1 small lemon

salt and ground black pepper

pitted and sliced black olives or salted capers, to garnish

1 Dip the bread briefly in cold water, then carefully squeeze out the excess water. Arrange the bread in the bottom of a shallow salad bowl.

2 Soak the onion slices in cold water for about 10 minutes while you prepare the other ingredients. Drain and reserve.

3 Layer the tomatoes, cheese, onion, basil or marjoram, seasoning well in between each layer. Sprinkle with oil, vinegar and lemon juice.

4 Top with the olives or capers, cover with plastic wrap and chill in the refrigerator for at least 2 hours or overnight, if possible.

Orange and Red Onion Salad with Cumin

Cumin and mint give this refreshing salad a Middle Eastern flavor. Choose small seedless oranges.

INGREDIENTS

INGREDIENTS

Serves 6

6 oranges

2 red onions

1 tablespoon cumin seeds

1 teaspoon coarsely ground black pepper

1 tablespoon chopped fresh mint

6 tablespoons olive oil

salt

To serve

fresh mint sprigs

black olives

1 Slice the oranges thinly, working over a bowl to catch any juice. Then, holding each orange slice in turn over the bowl, cut around with scissors to remove the peel and pith. Slice the onions thinly and separate the rings.

2 Arrange the orange and onion slices in layers in a shallow dish, sprinkling each layer with cumin seeds, black pepper, mint, olive oil and salt to taste. Pour on the orange juice collected when slicing the oranges.

3 Let the salad marinate in a cool place for about 2 hours. Just before serving, sprinkle on the mint sprigs and black olives.

Spanish Salad with Olives and Capers

Make this refreshing salad in the summer when tomatoes are sweet and full of flavor. The dressing gives it a great tang.

INGREDIENTS

Serves 4

4 tomatoes

½ cucumber

1 bunch scallions

1 bunch purslane or watercress, washed

8 pimiento-stuffed olives

2 tablespoons drained capers

Dressing

2 tablespoons red wine vinegar

1 teaspoon paprika

½ teaspoon ground cumin

1 garlic clove, crushed

5 tablespoons olive oil

salt and ground black pepper

1 To peel the tomatoes, place them in a heatproof bowl, add boiling water to cover and leave for 1 minute. Lift out with a slotted spoon and plunge into a bowl of cold water. Leave for 1 minute, then drain. Slip the skins off the tomatoes and dice the flesh finely. Put in a salad bowl.

2 Peel the cucumber, dice it finely and add it to the tomatoes. Trim and chop half the scallions, add them to the salad bowl and mix lightly.

3 Break the purslane or watercress into small sprigs. Add to the tomato mixture, with the olives and capers.

4 Make the dressing. Mix the wine vinegar, paprika, cumin and garlic in a bowl. Whisk in the oil and add salt and pepper to taste. Pour onto the salad and toss lightly to coat. Serve with the remaining scallions on the side.

Caesar Salad

*This is a well-known and much
enjoyed salad, even though its
origins are a mystery. Be sure to use
Romaine lettuce and add the very
soft eggs at the last minute.*

Serves 6

¾ cup salad oil, preferably olive oil

4 ounces French or Italian bread, cut in
  1-inch cubes

1 large garlic clove, crushed with the flat
  side of a knife

1 head Romaine lettuce

2 eggs, boiled for 1 minute

½ cup lemon juice

⅔ cup freshly grated Parmesan cheese

6 anchovy fillets, drained and finely
  chopped (optional)

salt and ground black pepper

1 Heat ¼ cup of the oil in a large
frying pan. Add the bread
cubes and garlic. Fry, stirring and
turning constantly, until the cubes
are golden brown all over. Drain
on paper towels. Discard the garlic.

2 Tear large lettuce leaves into
smaller pieces. Then put all the
lettuce in a bowl.

3 Add the remaining oil to the
lettuce and season with salt
and plenty of ground black pepper.
Toss well to coat the leaves.

4 Break the eggs on top. Sprinkle
with the lemon juice. Toss well
again to combine.

5 Add the Parmesan cheese and
anchovies, if using. Toss gently
to mix.

6 Sprinkle the fried bread cubes
on top and serve immediately.

COOK'S TIP

To make a tangier dressing mix
2 tablespoons white wine vinegar,
1 tablespoon Worcestershire
sauce, ½ teaspoon mustard
powder, 1 teaspoon sugar, salt
and pepper in a screw-top jar,
then add the oil and shake well.

Tricolor Salad

A popular salad, this dish depends for its success on the quality of its ingredients. Mozzarella di bufala is the best cheese to serve uncooked. Whole ripe plum tomatoes release their juices to blend with extra virgin olive oil for a natural dressing.

INGREDIENTS

Serves 2–3

5 ounces mozzarella di bufala cheese, thinly sliced

4 large plum tomatoes, sliced

1 large avocado

about 12 basil leaves or a small handful of flat-leaf parsley leaves

3–4 tablespoons extra virgin olive oil

ground black pepper

ciabatta and sea salt flakes, to serve

1 Arrange the sliced mozzarella cheese and tomatoes randomly on two salad plates. Crush on a few good pinches of sea salt flakes. This will help to draw out some of the juices from the plum tomatoes. Set aside in a cool place and let marinate for about 30 minutes.

2 Just before serving, cut the avocado in half using a large sharp knife and twist the halves to separate. Lift out the pit and remove the peel.

3 Carefully slice the avocado flesh crosswise into half moons, or cut it into large chunks, if that is easier.

4 Place the avocado on the salad, then sprinkle with the basil or parsley. Drizzle on the olive oil, add a little more salt if desired and some black pepper. Serve at room temperature, with chunks of crusty Italian ciabatta for mopping up the dressing.

Warm Fava Bean and Feta Salad

This recipe is loosely based on a typical medley of fresh-tasting Greek salad ingredients—fava beans, tomatoes and feta cheese. It's perfect as an appetizer, served warm or cold.

INGREDIENTS

Serves 4–6

2 pounds fava beans, shelled, or
    12 ounces shelled frozen beans

4 tablespoons olive oil

3 ounces plum tomatoes, halved, or
    quartered if large

4 garlic cloves, crushed

4 ounces firm feta cheese, cut into large,
    even-size chunks

3 tablespoons chopped fresh dill, plus
    extra to garnish

12 black olives

salt and ground black pepper

1 Cook the fresh or frozen fava beans in boiling, salted water until just tender. Drain and refresh, then set aside.

2 Meanwhile, heat the oil in a heavy frying pan and add the tomatoes and garlic. Cook until the tomatoes are beginning to color.

3 Add the feta to the pan and toss the ingredients together for 1 minute. Mix with the drained beans, dill, olives and salt and pepper. Serve garnished with chopped dill.

Halloumi and Grape Salad

In Eastern Europe, firm salty halloumi cheese is often served fried for breakfast or supper. In this recipe for an unusual appetizer it's tossed with sweet, juicy grapes, which really complement its distinctive sweet and salty flavor.

INGREDIENTS

Serves 4

5 ounces mixed salad greens

3 ounces seedless green grapes

3 ounces seedless black grapes

9 ounces halloumi cheese

3 tablespoons olive oil

fresh young thyme leaves or dill,
    to garnish

For the Dressing

4 tablespoons olive oil

1 tablespoon lemon juice

½ teaspoon sugar

salt and ground black pepper

1 teaspoon chopped fresh thyme or dill

1 To make the dressing, combine the olive oil, lemon juice and sugar. Season with salt and ground black pepper. Stir in the thyme or dill and set aside.

2 Toss together the salad greens and the green and black grapes, then transfer to a large serving plate.

3 Thinly slice the cheese. Heat the oil in a large frying pan. Add the cheese and fry briefly until turning golden on the underside. Turn the cheese with a spatula and cook the other side.

4 Arrange the cheese on the salad. Pour on the dressing and garnish with thyme or dill.

Asparagus and Orange Salad

A simple dressing of olive oil and vinegar mingles with the orange and tomato flavors with great results.

INGREDIENTS

Serves 4

8 ounces asparagus, trimmed and cut into
    2-inch pieces
2 large oranges
2 well-flavored ripe tomatoes, cut
    into eighths
2 ounces romaine lettuce leaves, shredded
2 tablespoons extra virgin olive oil
½ teaspoon sherry vinegar
salt and ground black pepper

1 Cook the asparagus in boiling, salted water for 3–4 minutes, until just tender. Drain and refresh under cold water. Set aside.

2 Grate the zest from half an orange and reserve. Peel all the oranges and cut into segments, leaving the membrane behind. Squeeze out the juice from the membrane and reserve the juice.

3 Put the asparagus, orange segments, tomatoes and lettuce into a salad bowl. Combine the oil and vinegar and add 1 tablespoon of the reserved orange juice and 1 teaspoon of the rind. Season with salt and plenty of ground black pepper. Just before serving, pour the dressing onto the salad and mix gently to coat.

Salade Niçoise

Made with the freshest ingredients, this classic Provençal salad makes a simple yet unbeatable summer dish. Serve with country-style bread and chilled white wine for a substantial appetizer.

INGREDIENTS

Serves 4–6

4 ounces green beans

1 tuna steak, about 6 ounces

olive oil, for brushing

4 ounces mixed salad greens

$\frac{1}{2}$ small cucumber, thinly sliced

4 ripe tomatoes, quartered

2-ounce can anchovies, drained and
    halved lengthwise

4 hard-boiled eggs, quartered

$\frac{1}{2}$ bunch radishes, trimmed

$\frac{1}{2}$ cup small black olives

salt and ground black pepper

flat-leaf parsley, to garnish

For the dressing

6 tablespoons virgin olive oil

2 garlic cloves, crushed

1 tablespoon white wine vinegar

salt and ground black pepper

1 Whisk together the oil, garlic and vinegar then season to taste with salt and pepper.

2 Preheat the broiler. Brush the tuna steak with olive oil and season with salt and black pepper. Broil for 3–4 minutes on each side, until cooked through. Set aside and let cool.

3 Trim and halve the beans. Cook them in a pan of boiling water for 2 minutes, until only just tender, then drain, refresh and let cool.

4 Combine the salad greens, sliced cucumber, tomatoes and beans in a large, shallow bowl. Flake the tuna steak with your fingers or two forks.

5 Sprinkle the tuna, anchovies, eggs, radishes and olives on the salad. Pour on the dressing and toss lightly. Serve garnished with parsley.

Pear and Roquefort Salad

Choose ripe, firm Comice or Williams pears for this salad.

Serves 4

3 ripe pears

lemon juice, for tossing

about 6 ounces mixed salad greens

6 ounces Roquefort cheese

1/2 cup hazelnuts, toasted and chopped

For the dressing

2 tablespoons hazelnut oil

3 tablespoons olive oil

1 tablespoon cider vinegar

1 teaspoon Dijon mustard

salt and ground black pepper

1 To make the dressing, combine the oils, vinegar and mustard in a bowl or screw-top jar. Add salt and black pepper to taste. Stir or shake well.

2 Peel, core and slice the pears and toss them in lemon juice.

3 Arrange the salad greens on serving plates, then place the pears on top. Crumble the cheese onto the salad with the hazelnuts. Spoon on the dressing and serve immediately.

Green Bean and Sweet Red Bell Pepper Salad

Serrano chiles are very fiery so be cautious when using them.

Serves 4

12 ounces cooked green beans, quartered

2 red bell peppers, seeded and chopped

2 scallions, chopped

1 or more drained pickled serrano chiles, rinsed, seeded and chopped

1 iceberg lettuce, coarsely shredded

olives, to garnish

For the dressing

3 tablespoons red wine vinegar

9 tablespoons olive oil

salt and ground black pepper

1 Combine the cooked green beans, chopped peppers, chopped scallions and chiles in a salad bowl.

2 Make the salad dressing. Pour the red wine vinegar into a bowl. Add salt and ground black pepper to taste, then gradually whisk in the olive oil until well combined.

3 Pour the salad dressing onto the prepared vegetables and toss lightly together to mix and coat thoroughly.

4 Line a large serving platter with the shredded iceberg lettuce leaves and arrange the salad vegetables attractively on top. Garnish with the olives and serve.

Wilted Spinach and Bacon Salad

The hot dressing in this salad wilts the spinach and provides a taste sensation.

INGREDIENTS

Serves 6

1 pound fresh young spinach leaves

8 ounces bacon

1½ tablespoon vegetable oil

4 tablespoons red wine vinegar

4 tablespoons water

4 teaspoons sugar

1 teaspoon dry mustard

8 scallions, thinly sliced

6 radishes, thinly sliced

2 hard-boiled eggs, coarsely grated

salt and ground black pepper

1 Pull any coarse stalks from the spinach leaves and rinse well. Put the leaves in a large salad bowl.

2 Fry the bacon in the oil until crisp and brown. Remove with tongs and drain on paper towels. Reserve the cooking fat in the pan. Chop the bacon and set aside until needed.

3 Combine the vinegar, water, sugar, mustard, and salt and ground black pepper in a bowl and stir until smoothly blended. Add to the fat in the frying pan and stir to mix. Bring the dressing to a boil, stirring.

4 Pour the hot dressing evenly on the spinach leaves. Sprinkle on the bacon, scallions, radishes and eggs, and toss, then serve.

Melon and Prosciutto Salad

Sections of cool fragrant melon wrapped with slices of prosciutto make a delicious salad. If strawberries are in season, serve with a savory-sweet strawberry salsa and watch it disappear.

Serves 4

1 large melon, cantaloupe, charentais or galia

6 ounces prosciutto, thinly sliced

For the salsa

2 cups strawberries

1 teaspoon sugar

2 tablespoon peanut or sunflower oil

1 tablespoon orange juice

$\frac{1}{2}$ teaspoon finely grated orange zest

$\frac{1}{2}$ teaspoon finely grated fresh ginger

salt and ground black pepper

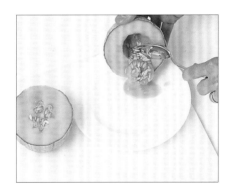

1 Halve the melon and scoop the seeds out with a spoon. Cut the zest off with a paring knife, then slice the melon thickly. Chill until ready to serve.

2 To make the salsa, hull the strawberries and cut them into large dice. Place in a small mixing bowl with the sugar and crush lightly to release the juices. Add the oil, orange juice, zest and ginger. Season with salt and plenty of ground black pepper.

3 Arrange the melon on a serving plate, lay the prosciutto on top and serve with a bowl of salsa.

Roasted Tomato and Mozzarella Salad

Roasting the tomatoes brings out their sweetness and adds a new dimension to this salad. Make the basil oil just before serving to retain its fresh flavor and vivid color.

INGREDIENTS

Serves 4

6 large plum tomatoes

olive oil, for brushing

2 fresh mozzarella cheese balls, cut into
    8–12 slices

salt and ground black pepper

basil leaves, to garnish

For the basil oil

25 basil leaves

4 tablespoons extra virgin olive oil

1 garlic clove, crushed

1 Preheat the oven to 400°F and oil a baking sheet. Cut the tomatoes in half lengthwise and remove the seeds. Place the halves skin-side down on the baking sheet and roast for 20 minutes or until the tomatoes are very tender but still retain their shape.

2 Meanwhile, make the basil oil. Place the basil leaves, olive oil and garlic in a food processor or blender and process until smooth. You will need to scrape down the sides once or twice to ensure that the mixture is processed properly. Transfer to a bowl and chill until needed.

3 For each serving, place the tomato halves on top of 2 or 3 slices of mozzarella and drizzle on the oil. Season well. Garnish with basil leaves and serve immediately.

Mixed Herb Salad with Toasted Mixed Seeds

This simple salad is the perfect antidote to a rich, heavy meal as it contains fresh herbs that can ease the digestion. Balsamic vinegar adds a rich, sweet taste to the dressing, but red or white wine vinegar could be used instead.

INGREDIENTS

Serves 4

4 cups mixed salad greens

2 cups mixed salad herbs, such as cilantro,
    parsley, basil, and chervil

3 tablespoons pumpkin seeds

3 tablespoons sunflower seeds

For the dressing

4 tablespoons extra virgin olive oil

1 tablespoon balsamic vinegar

½ teaspoon Dijon mustard

salt and ground black pepper

1 To make the dressing, combine the ingredients in a bowl or screw-top jar. Mix with a small whisk or fork, or shake well, until completely combined.

2 Put the salad greens and herb leaves in a large bowl. Toss with your fingers.

3 Toast the pumpkin and sunflower seeds in a dry frying pan over medium heat for about 2 minutes, until golden, tossing frequently to prevent them from burning. Let the seeds cool slightly before sprinkling them on the salad.

4 Pour the dressing onto the salad and toss with your hands until the leaves are well coated, then serve.

Potato Salad with Curry Mayonnaise

Potato salad can be made well in advance and is therefore a useful dish for serving as an unusual appetizer at a party. Its popularity means that there are very rarely any leftovers to be cleared at the end of the day.

INGREDIENTS

Serves 6

2¼ pounds new potatoes, in skins

1¼ cups mayonnaise

1 tablespoon curry powder

salt and ground black pepper

mixed lettuce leaves or other salad greens, to serve

1 Place the potatoes in a pan of salted water, bring to a boil and cook for 15 minutes or until tender. Drain and place in a large bowl to cool slightly.

2 Mix the mayonnaise with the curry and black pepper. Stir into the potatoes while they are still warm. Let cool completely, then serve on a bed of mixed lettuce leaves or other assorted salad greens.

Avocado and Smoked Fish Salad

Avocado and smoked fish make a good combination and, flavored with herbs and spices, create a delectable and elegant salad.

Serves 4

1 tablespoon butter or margarine

½ onion, finely sliced

1 teaspoon mustard seeds

8 ounces smoked mackerel, flaked

2 tablespoons fresh chopped cilantro

2 firm tomatoes, peeled and chopped

1 tablespoon lemon juice

For the salad

2 avocados

½ cucumber

1 tablespoon lemon juice

2 firm tomatoes

1 green chile

salt and ground black pepper

1 Melt the butter or margarine in a frying pan, add the onion and mustard seeds and fry for about 5 minutes, until the onion is soft but not browned.

2 Add the fish, chopped cilantro, tomatoes and lemon juice and cook over low heat for 2–3 minutes. Remove from the heat and let cool.

COOK'S TIP

Smoked mackerel has a distinctive flavor, but smoked haddock or cod can also be used in this salad or a mixture of mackerel and haddock. For a speedy salad, canned tuna makes a convenient substitute.

3 To make the salad, slice the avocados and cucumber thinly. Place together in a bowl and sprinkle with the lemon juice to prevent discoloration.

4 Slice the tomatoes and seed and finely chop the chile.

5 Place the fish mixture in the center of a serving plate.

6 Arrange the avocado slices, cucumber and tomatoes decoratively around the outside of the fish. Alternatively, spoon a quarter of the fish mixture onto each of four serving plates and divide the avocados, cucumber and tomatoes equally among them. Then sprinkle with the chopped chile and a little salt and ground black pepper, and serve.

Piquant Shrimp Salad

The Thai-inspired dressing, which includes fish sauce and sesame oil, adds a superb flavor to the rice noodles and tiger shrimp. This delicious salad can be served warm; or alternatively, chill before serving.

INGREDIENTS

Serves 6

7 ounces rice vermicelli or stir-fry
   rice noodles

8 ears baby corn, halved

5 ounces snowpeas

1 tablespoon stir-fry oil

2 garlic cloves, finely chopped

1-inch piece fresh ginger, peeled and
   finely chopped

1 fresh red or green chile, seeded and
   finely chopped

1 pound peeled tiger shrimp

4 scallions, very thinly sliced

1 tablespoon sesame seeds, toasted

1 lemongrass stalk, thinly shredded,
   to garnish

For the dressing

1 tablespoon snipped fresh chives

1 tablespoon *nam pla* (Thai fish sauce)

1 teaspoon soy sauce

3 tablespoons peanut oil

1 teaspoon sesame oil

2 tablespoons rice vinegar

1 Put the rice vermicelli or noodles in a wide heatproof bowl, pour on boiling water and leave for 5 minutes. Drain, refresh under cold water and drain again. Put back in the bowl and set aside until required.

2 Boil or steam the corn and snowpeas for about 3 minutes; they should still be crunchy. Refresh under cold water and drain. Now make the dressing. Mix all the ingredients in a screw-top jar, close tightly and shake well to combine.

3 Heat the oil in a large frying pan or wok. Add the garlic, ginger and red or green chile and cook for 1 minute. Add the tiger shrimp and stir-fry for 3 minutes, until they have just turned pink. Add the scallions, corn, snowpeas and sesame seeds, and toss lightly to mix.

4 Put the contents of the pan or wok over the rice vermicelli or noodles. Pour the dressing on top and toss well. Serve, garnished with lemongrass, or chill for an hour before serving.

Mushroom Salad with Prosciutto

Ribbons of crêpe create texture in this appetizer. Use whatever edible wild mushrooms you can find, or substitute interesting cultivated varieties if you need to.

Serves 4

3 tablespoons unsalted butter

1 pound assorted wild and cultivated
  mushrooms such as chanterelles, cêpes,
  bay boletus, Caesar's mushrooms,
  oyster, field and Paris mushrooms,
  trimmed and sliced

4 tablespoons Madeira or sherry

juice of ½ lemon

½ oak leaf lettuce

½ frisée lettuce

2 tablespoons walnut oil

salt and ground black pepper

For the crêpe ribbons

3 tablespoons all-purpose flour

5 tablespoons milk

1 egg

4 tablespoons freshly grated
  Parmesan cheese

4 tablespoons chopped fresh herbs such as
  parsley, thyme, marjoram or chives

salt and pepper

butter, for frying

6 ounces prosciutto, thickly sliced

1 To make the crêpes, blend the flour and the milk. Beat in the egg, cheese, herbs and some seasoning. Heat the butter in a frying pan and pour enough of the mixture to coat the bottom. When the batter has set, turn the crêpe over and cook until firm.

2 Turn out and cool. Roll up the crêpe and slice thinly to make ½-inch ribbons. Cook the remaining batter in the same way and cut the prosciutto into similar sized ribbons. Toss with the crêpe ribbons. Set aside.

3 Gently soften the mushrooms in the remaining butter for 6–8 minutes, until the moisture has evaporated. Add the Madeira or sherry and lemon juice; season.

4 Toss the salad greens in the oil and arrange on four plates. Place the prosciutto and crêpe ribbons in the center, spoon on the mushrooms and serve.

Goat Cheese Salad

Goat cheese has a strong, tangy flavor so choose robust salad greens to accompany it.

INGREDIENTS

Serves 4

2 tablespoons olive oil

4 slices of French bread, ½-inch thick

8 cups mixed salad greens, such as curly endive, radicchio and red oak leaf, torn in small pieces

4 firm goat cheese rounds, about 2 ounces each, rind removed

1 yellow or red bell pepper, seeded and finely diced

1 small red onion, thinly sliced

3 tablespoons chopped fresh parsley

2 tablespoons snipped fresh chives

For the dressing

2 tablespoonss white wine vinegar

¼ teaspoon salt

1 teaspoon whole-grain mustard

5 tablespoons olive oil

ground black pepper

1 For the dressing, mix the vinegar and salt with a fork until dissolved. Stir in the mustard. Gradually stir in the olive oil until blended. Season with pepper and set aside until needed.

2 Preheat the broiler. Heat the oil in a skillet. When hot, add the bread slices and fry until golden, about 1 minute. Turn and cook on the other side, about 30 more seconds more. Drain on paper towels and set aside.

3 Place the salad greens in a bowl. Add 3 tablespoons of the dressing and toss to coat well. Divide the dressed leaves among four salad plates.

4 Preheat the broiler. Place the goat cheeses, cut sides up, on a baking sheet and broil until bubbling and golden, 1–2 minutes.

5 Set a goat cheese on each slice of bread and place in the center of each plate. Sprinkle the diced pepper, red onion, parsley and chives on the salad. Drizzle with the remaining dressing and serve.

Smoked Trout Pasta Salad

The little pasta shells catch the trout, creating tasty mouthfuls.

Serves 8

1 tablespoon butter

1 cup minced fennel

6 scallions, 2 minced and the rest
   thinly sliced

8 ounces skinless smoked trout
   fillets, flaked

3 tablespoons chopped fresh dill

½ cup mayonnaise

2 teaspoons fresh lemon juice

2 tablespoons whipping cream

4 cups small pasta shapes, such as
   conchiglie

salt and ground black pepper

dill sprigs, to garnish

1 Melt the butter in a small pan. Cook the fennel and minced onions for 3–5 minutes. Transfer to a large bowl and cool slightly.

2 Add the sliced scallions, trout, dill, mayonnaise, lemon juice and cream. Season and mix.

3 Bring a large pan of water to a boil. Salt to taste and add the pasta. Cook according to the instructions on the package until just *al dente*. Drain thoroughly and let cool.

4 Add the pasta to the vegetable and trout mixture and toss to coat evenly. Taste for seasoning. Serve the salad lightly chilled or at room temperature, garnished with sprigs of dill.

Mixed Seafood Salad

If you cannot find all the seafood included in this dish in fresh form, then it's all right to use a combination of fresh and frozen, but do use what is in season first.

INGREDIENTS

Serves 6–8

12 ounces small squid

1 small onion, cut into quarters

1 bay leaf

7 ounces unpeeled shrimp

1½ pound fresh mussels, in the shell

1 pound small fresh clams

¾ cup white wine

1 fennel bulb

For the dressing

5 tablespoons extra virgin olive oil

3 tablespoons lemon juice

1 garlic clove, finely chopped

salt and ground black pepper

1 Working near the sink, clean the squid by first peeling off the thin skin from the body section. Rinse well. Pull the head and tentacles away from the sac section. Some of the intestines will come away with the head. Remove and discard the translucent quill and any remaining insides from the sac. Sever the tentacles from the head. Discard the head and intestines. Remove the small hard beak from the base of the tentacles. Rinse the sac and tentacles of the squid well under cold running water. Drain in a colander.

2 Bring a large pan of water to a boil. Add the onion and bay leaf. Drop in the squid and cook for about 10 minutes or until tender. Remove with a draining spoon, and let cool before slicing into rings ½-inch wide. Cut each tentacle section into 2 pieces. Set aside.

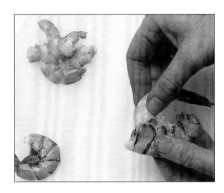

3 Drop the shrimp into the same boiling water, and cook until they turn pink, about 2 minutes. Remove with a draining spoon. Peel and devein. (The cooking liquid may be strained and kept for using to make soup.) When cool, pop into the freezer if not using immediately.

4 Cut off the "beards" from the mussels. Scrub and rinse the mussels and clams well in several changes of cold water. Place in a large saucepan with the wine. Cover, and steam until all the shells have opened. (Discard any that do not open.) Lift the clams and mussels out.

5 Remove all the clams from their shells with a small spoon. Place in a large serving bowl. Remove all but 8 of the mussels from their shells, and add them to the clams in the bowl. Leave the remaining mussels in their half shells, and set aside. Cut the green, ferny part of the fennel off the bulb. Chop finely and set aside. Chop the bulb into bite-size pieces, and add it to the serving bowl with the squid and shrimp.

6 Make a dressing by combining the oil, lemon juice, garlic and chopped fennel green in a small bowl. Add salt and pepper to taste. Pour onto the salad, and toss well. Decorate with the remaining mussels in the half shell. This salad may be served either at room temperature or lightly chilled.

Egg and Fennel Tabbouleh with Nuts

Tabbouleh is a Middle Eastern salad of steamed bulghur wheat, flavored with lots of parsley, mint and garlic.

INGREDIENTS

Serves 4

1¼ cups bulghur wheat

4 small eggs

1 fennel bulb

1 bunch scallions, chopped

½ cup sun-dried tomatoes, sliced

3 tablespoons chopped fresh parsley

2 tablespoons chopped fresh mint

½ cup black olives

4 tablespoons olive oil, preferably Greek
    or Spanish

2 tablespoons garlic oil

2 tablespoons lemon juice

salt and ground black pepper

1 Cover the bulghur wheat with boiling water and let soak for 15 minutes. Transfer to a metal sieve, place over a saucepan of boiling water, cover and steam for 10 minutes. Spread out on a metal tray and let cool while you cook the eggs and fennel.

2 Hard-boil the small eggs for 8 minutes. Cool under running water, peel and quarter or, using an egg slicer, slice not quite all the way through.

3 Halve and then finely slice the fennel. Boil in salted water for 6 minutes, drain and cool under running water.

4 Combine the egg quarters, fennel, scallions, sun-dried tomatoes, parsley, mint and olives with the bulghur wheat. If you have sliced the eggs, arrange them on top of the salad. Dress the tabbouleh with olive oil, garlic oil and lemon juice. Season well.

COOK'S TIP

Small whole eggs, such as gull, quail, plover or guinea fowl, would be good in this dish.

Ceviche

You can use almost any firm-fleshed fish for this South American dish, provided that is perfectly fresh. The fish is "cooked" by the action of the acidic lime juice. Adjust the amount of chile according to your taste.

INGREDIENTS

Serves 6

1½ pounds halibut, turbot, sea bass or
   salmon fillets, skinned

juice of 3 limes

1–2 fresh red chiles, seeded and very finely
   chopped

1 tablespoon olive oil

salt, to taste

For the garnish

4 large firm tomatoes, peeled, seeded
   and diced

1 ripe avocado, peeled and diced

1 tablespoon lemon juice

2 tablespoons olive oil

2 tablespoons fresh cilantro leaves

1 Cut the fish into strips measuring about 2 x ½ inches. Lay these in a shallow dish and pour on the lime juice, turning the fish strips to coat them all over in the juice. Cover with plastic wrap and leave for 1 hour.

2 Meanwhile, prepare the garnish. Combine all the ingredients except the cilantro. Set aside.

3 Season the fish with salt and sprinkle on the chiles. Drizzle with the olive oil. Toss the fish in the mixture, then replace the cover. Let marinate in the refrigerator for 15–30 more minutes. To serve, divide the garnish among six plates. Arrange the ceviche, then sprinkle with cilantro.

PARTY FINGER FOOD

Cheese Aigrettes

Choux pastry is often associated with sweet pastries, such as profiteroles, but these little savory buns, flavored with Gruyère and dusted with grated Parmesan, are just delicious. They are best made ahead and deep-fried to serve. They make a wonderful party snack.

INGREDIENTS

Makes 30

scant 1 cup all-purpose flour
½ teaspoon paprika
½ teaspoon salt
6 tablespoons cold butter, diced
scant 1 cup water
3 eggs, beaten
3 ounces aged Gruyère cheese,
    coarsely grated
corn or vegetable oil, for deep-frying
⅔ cup freshly grated Parmesan cheese
ground black pepper

1 Combine the flour, paprika and salt by sifting them onto a large sheet of waxed paper. Add a generous amount of ground black pepper.

2 Put the diced butter and water into a medium saucepan and heat gently. As soon as the butter has melted and the liquid starts to boil, quickly put in all the seasoned flour at once and beat very hard with a wooden spoon until the dough comes away cleanly from the sides of the pan.

3 Remove the saucepan from the heat and cool the paste for 5 minutes. Gradually beat in enough of the beaten egg to give a stiff dropping consistency that still holds a shape on the spoon. Mix in the Gruyère.

4 Heat the oil for deep-frying to 350°F. Take a teaspoonful of the choux paste and use a second spoon to slide it into the oil. Make more aigrettes in the same way. Fry for 3–4 minutes, then drain on paper towels and keep warm while cooking successive batches. To serve, pile the aigrettes on a warmed serving dish and sprinkle with Parmesan.

COOK'S TIP

Filling these aigrettes gives a delightful surprise as you bite through their crisp shell. Make slightly larger aigrettes by dropping a slightly larger spoonful of dough into the hot oil. Slit them open and scoop out any soft paste. Fill the centers with taramasalata or crumbled Roquefort mixed with a little fromage frais.

Parmesan Thins

These thin, crisp, savory crackers will melt in your mouth, so make plenty for guests. They are a great snack at any time of the day, so don't just keep them for parties.

INGREDIENTS

Makes 16–20

½ cup all-purpose flour

3 tablespoons butter, softened

1 egg yolk

⅔ cup freshly grated Parmesan cheese

pinch of salt

pinch of mustard powder

1 Rub together the flour and the butter in a bowl using your fingertips, then work in the egg yolk, Parmesan cheese, salt and mustard. Mix to bring the dough together into a ball. Shape the mixture into a log, wrap in aluminum foil or plastic wrap and chill in the refrigerator for 10 minutes.

2 Preheat the oven to 400°F. Cut the Parmesan log into very thin slices, ⅛–¼ inch maximum, and arrange on a baking sheet. Flatten with a fork to give a pretty ridged pattern. Bake for 10 minutes or until the crackers are crisp but not changing color.

Broiled Polenta with Gorgonzola

Broiled polenta is delicious, and is a good way of using up cold polenta. Try it with any soft flavorful cheese. Here the polenta is cut into triangles but you could make different shapes if desired.

INGREDIENTS

Serves 6–8

6¼ cups water

1 tablespoon salt

2½ cups cornmeal

1¼ cups Gorgonzola or other cheese, at
 room temperature

1 Bring the water to a boil in a large heavy saucepan. Add the salt. Reduce the water to simmering, and begin to add the cornmeal in a fine rain. Stir constantly with a whisk until the cornmeal has all been incorporated.

2 Switch to a long-handled wooden spoon, and continue to stir the polenta over low to medium heat until it is a thick mass and pulls away from the sides of the pan. This may take from 25–50 minutes, depending on the type of cornmeal used. For best results, never stop stirring the polenta until you remove it from the heat.

3 When the polenta is cooked, sprinkle a work surface or large board with a little water. Spread the polenta out on the surface in a layer ¾ inch thick. Let cool completely. Preheat the broiler.

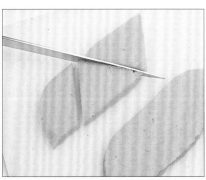

4 Cut the polenta into triangles. Broil until hot and speckled with brown on both sides. Spread with the Gorgonzola or other cheese. Serve immediately.

Cherry Tomatoes with Pesto

These make a colorful and tasty appetizer to go with drinks before you move to the table. Make the pesto when fresh basil is plentiful, and freeze it in batches.

INGREDIENTS

Serves 8–10

1 pound small cherry tomatoes

For the pesto

1 cup fresh basil leaves

3–4 garlic cloves

4 tablespoons pine nuts

1 teaspoon salt, plus extra to taste

½ cup olive oil

3 tablespoons freshly grated
    Parmesan cheese

6 tablespoons freshly grated
    pecorino cheese

ground black pepper

1 Wash the tomatoes. Slice off the top of each tomato, and carefully scoop out the seeds with a melon baller or small spoon.

2 Place the basil, garlic, pine nuts, salt and olive oil in a blender or food processor and process until smooth. Remove the contents to a bowl with a rubber spatula. If desired, the pesto may be frozen at this point, before the cheeses are added. To use when frozen, let thaw, then proceed to step 3.

3 Fold in the Parmesan and pecorino grated cheeses. Season with pepper, and more salt if necessary.

4 Use a small spoon to fill each tomato with a little pesto. This dish is at its best if chilled for about an hour before serving.

Spicy Peanut Balls

Tasty rice balls, rolled in chopped peanuts and deep-fried, make a delicious appetizer. Serve them as they are, or with a chili sauce for dipping. Make sure there are plenty of napkins on hand.

INGREDIENTS

Makes 16

1 garlic clove, crushed

½-inch piece fresh ginger, peeled and finely chopped

¼ teaspoon turmeric

1 teaspoon sugar

½ teaspoon salt

1 teaspoon chili sauce

2 teaspoons fish sauce or soy sauce

2 tablespoons chopped cilantro

juice of ½ lime

2 cups cooked white long grain rice

1 cup peanuts, chopped

vegetable oil, for deep-frying

lime wedges and chili dipping sauce, to serve (optional)

1 Process the garlic, ginger and turmeric in a food processor or blender until the mixture forms a paste. Add the sugar, salt, chili sauce and fish sauce or soy sauce, with the chopped cilantro and lime juice. Process briefly to mix the ingredients.

2 Add three-quarters of the cooked rice to the paste in the and process until smooth and sticky. Scrape into a mixing bowl and stir in the remainder of the rice. Wet your hands and shape the mixture into thumb-size balls.

3 Roll the balls in the chopped peanuts, making sure they are evenly coated.

4 Heat the oil in a deep-fryer or wok. Deep-fry the peanut balls until crisp. Drain on paper towels and then pile onto a platter. Serve hot with lime wedges and a chili dipping sauce, if using.

Eggs Mimosa

The use of the word mimosa describes the fine yellow and white grated egg, which looks not unlike the flower of the same name. It can be used to finish any dish, adding a light summery touch.

Serves 20

12 hard-boiled eggs, peeled

2 ripe avocados, halved and pitted

1 garlic clove, crushed

Tabasco sauce, to taste

1 tablespoon virgin olive oil

salt and ground black pepper

20 endive leaves or small crisp green
   lettuce leaves, to serve

basil leaves, to garnish

1 Reserve 2 eggs, halve the remainder and put the yolks in a mixing bowl. Blend or beat the yolks with the avocados, garlic, Tabasco sauce, oil and salt and pepper. Check the seasoning. Pipe or spoon this mixture back into the halved egg whites.

2 Sieve the remaining egg whites and sprinkle on the filled eggs. Sieve the yolks on top. Arrange each half egg on an endive or lettuce leaf and place them on a serving platter. Sprinkle the shredded basil on the filled egg halves before serving.

Pickled Quail's Eggs

These Chinese eggs are pickled in alcohol and can be stored in a preserving jar in a cool dark place for several months. They will make delicious bite-size snacks at a cocktail party and are sure to delight guests.

INGREDIENTS

Serves 12

12 quail's eggs

1 tablespoon salt

3 cups distilled or previously boiled water

1 teaspoon Szechuan peppercorns

⅔ cup alcohol such as Mou-tal (Chinese brandy), brandy, whiskey, rum or vodka

dipping sauce (see Cook's Tip) and toasted sesame seeds, to serve

1 Boil the eggs for about 4 minutes, until the yolks are soft but not runny.

2 In a large saucepan, dissolve the salt in the distilled or previously boiled water. Add the peppercorns, then let the water cool and add the alcohol.

3 Gently tap the eggs all over but do not peel them. Place in a large, airtight, sterilized jar and fill up with the liquid, totally covering the eggs. Seal the jar and let the eggs stand in a cool, dark place for 7–8 days.

4 To serve, remove the eggs from the liquid and peel off the shells carefully. Cut each egg in half or quarters and serve whole with a dipping sauce and a bowl of toasted sesame seeds.

COOK'S TIP

• Although you can buy Chinese dipping sauces at the supermarket, it is very easy to make your own at home. To make a quick dipping sauce, mix equal amounts of soy sauce and hoisin sauce.

• Be sure to use only boiled water or distilled water for the eggs, as the water must be completely free of bacteria, or it will enter the porous shells.

Tandoori Chicken Sticks

This aromatic chicken dish is traditionally baked in a special clay oven called a tandoor. Here the chicken is broiled, with truly excellent results.

INGREDIENTS

Makes about 25

1 pound boneless, skinless chicken breasts

For the cilantro yogurt

1 cup plain yogurt

2 tablespoons whipping cream

½ cucumber, peeled, seeded and
  finely chopped

1–2 tablespoons fresh chopped cilantro

salt and ground black pepper

For the marinade

¾ cup plain yogurt

1 teaspoon garam masala or curry powder

¼ teaspoon ground cumin

¼ teaspoon ground coriander

¼ teaspoon cayenne pepper (or to taste)

1 teaspoon tomato paste

1–2 garlic cloves, finely chopped

1-inch piece fresh ginger, peeled and
  finely chopped

grated zest and juice of ½ lemon

1–2 tablespoons chopped fresh cilantro

1 Prepare the cilantro yogurt. Combine all the ingredients in a bowl and season with salt and ground black pepper. Cover with plastic wrap and chill until you are ready to serve.

2 Prepare the marinade. Place all the ingredients in the bowl of a food processor, and process until the mixture is smooth. Pour into a shallow dish.

3 Freeze the chicken breasts for 5 minutes to firm, then slice in half horizontally. Cut the slices into ¾-inch strips and add to the marinade. Toss to coat well. Cover and chill in the refrigerator for 6–8 hours or overnight.

4 Preheat the broiler and line a baking sheet with aluminum foil. Using a draining spoon, remove the chicken from the marinade and arrange the pieces in a single layer on the baking sheet. Scrunch up the chicken slightly so it makes wavy shapes. Broil for 4–5 minutes, until brown and just cooked, turning once. When cool enough to handle, thread 1–2 pieces onto cocktail sticks or skewers and serve with the cilantro yogurt dip.

Stuffed Deviled Eggs

These eggs are so simple to make, yet guests will always be impressed by them. They have a wonderful flavor and can be given quite a "kick" too by including the cayenne.

INGREDIENTS

Serves 6

6 hard-boiled eggs, peeled

¼ cup minced cooked ham

6 walnut halves, minced

1 tablespoon minced scallion

1 tablespoon Dijon mustard

1 tablespoon mayonnaise

2 teaspoons vinegar

¼ teaspoon salt

¼ teaspoon ground black pepper

¼ teaspoon cayenne pepper (optional)

paprika and a few gherkin slices,
    to garnish

1 Cut each hard-boiled egg in half lengthwise. Put the yolks in a bowl and set the whites aside.

2 Mash the yolks well with a fork, or push them through a sieve. Add all the remaining ingredients except the garnish and mix well with the yolks. Taste and add more salt and pepper seasoning if necessary.

3 Spoon the filling into the egg white halves, or pipe it in with a pastry bag and nozzle. Garnish the top of each stuffed egg with a little paprika and a small star or other shape cut from the pickle slices. Serve the stuffed eggs at room temperature.

Stuffed Celery Sticks

The creamy filling contrasts well with the crunchy celery, and the walnuts add a wonderful flavor.

INGREDIENTS

Serves 4–6

12 crisp, tender celery stalks

¼ cup crumbled blue cheese

½ cup cream cheese

3 tablespoons sour cream

½ cup chopped walnuts

1 Trim the celery stalks. Wash them, if necessary, and dry well on paper towels. Cut into 4-inch lengths.

2 In a small bowl, combine the crumbled blue cheese, cream cheese and sour cream. Stir together with a wooden spoon until smoothly blended. Fold in all but 1 tablespoon of the walnuts.

3 Fill the celery pieces with the cheese and nut mixture. Chill before serving, garnished with the reserved walnuts.

COOK'S TIP

Use the same filling to stuff scooped-out cherry tomatoes. Serve together, if desired.

Tapenade and Quail's Eggs

Tapenade is a purée made from capers, olives and anchovies. It is used in Mediterranean cooking. It complements the taste of eggs perfectly, especially quail's eggs, which look very pretty on open-face sandwiches.

INGREDIENTS

Serves 8

8 quail's eggs

1 small baguette

3 tablespoons tapenade

chicory leaves

3 small tomatoes, sliced

black olives

4 canned anchovy fillets, drained and
   halved lengthwise

parsley sprigs, to garnish

1 Boil the quail's eggs for 3 minutes, then plunge them straight into cold water to cool. Crack the shells and remove them very carefully.

2 Cut the baguette into slices on the diagonal and spread each one with some of the tapenade.

3 Arrange a little chicory, torn to fit, and the tomato slices, on top.

4 Halve the quail's eggs and place them on top of the tomato slices.

5 Finish with a little more tapenade, the olives and finally the anchovies. Garnish with small parsley sprigs.

COOK'S TIP

To make $1\frac{1}{4}$ cups of tuna tapenade, put $3\frac{1}{2}$ ounces canned drained tuna in a food processor with 2 tablespoons capers, 10 canned anchovy fillets and $\frac{3}{4}$ cup pitted black olives and blend until smooth, scraping down the sides as necessary. Gradually add 4 tablespoons olive oil through the feeder tube. This purée can be used for filling hard-boiled eggs. Blend the tapenade with the egg yolks, then pile into the whites.

Eggy Thai Fish Cakes

These tangy little fish cakes, with a kick of spice, make great party food or, made slightly larger, are a great appetizer too.

INGREDIENTS

Makes about 20

8 ounces smoked cod or haddock
   (undyed)

8 ounces fresh cod or haddock

1 small fresh red chile, seeded and
   finely chopped

2 garlic cloves, grated

1 lemongrass stalk, very finely chopped

2 large scallions, very finely chopped

2 tablespoons Thai fish sauce (or
   2 tablespoons soy sauce and a few drops
   anchovy extract)

4 tablespoons thick coconut milk

2 large eggs, lightly beaten

1 tablespoon chopped fresh cilantro

1 tablespoon cornstarch, plus extra
   for molding

oil, for frying

soy sauce, rice vinegar or Thai fish sauce,
   for dipping

1 Place the prepared smoked fish in a bowl of cold water and let soak for 10 minutes. Dry well on paper towels. Chop the smoked and fresh fish roughly and place in a food processor.

2 Add the chile, garlic, lemongrass, onions, the sauce and the coconut milk, and process until the fish is well blended with the spices. Add the eggs and cilantro and process for another few seconds. Cover with plastic wrap and chill in the refrigerator for 1 hour.

3 To make the fish cakes, flour your hands with cornstarch and shape large teaspoonfuls into neat balls, coating them with the flour.

4 Heat 2–3 inches oil in a medium pan until a crust of bread turns golden in about 1 minute. Fry the fish balls 5–6 at a time, turning them carefully with a slotted spoon for 2–3 minutes, until they turn golden all over. Remove with a slotted spoon and drain on paper towels. Keep the fish cakes warm in the oven until they are all cooked. Serve immediately with one or more dipping sauces.

Marinated Mussels

This is an ideal recipe to prepare and arrange well in advance. Remove from the refrigerator 15 minutes before serving to let the flavors develop fully.

INGREDIENTS

Makes about 48

2¼ pounds mussels, large if possible
    (about 48)
¾ cup dry white wine
1 garlic clove, finely crushed
½ cup olive oil
¼ cup lemon juice
1 teaspoon hot chile flakes
½ teaspoon allspice
1 tablespoon Dijon mustard
2 teaspoons sugar
1 teaspoon salt
1–2 tablespoons chopped fresh dill
    or cilantro
1 tablespoon capers, drained and chopped
    if large
ground black pepper

1 With a stiff kitchen brush, under cold running water, scrub the mussels to remove any sand and barnacles; pull off and remove the beards. Discard any open shells that will not shut when they are tapped.

2 In a large casserole or pan set over high heat, bring the white wine to a boil with the garlic and freshly ground black pepper. Add the mussels and cover. Reduce the heat to medium and simmer for 2–4 minutes, until the shells open, stirring occasionally.

3 In a large bowl combine the olive oil, lemon juice, chile flakes, allspice, Dijon mustard, sugar, salt, the chopped dill or cilantro and the capers. Stir well then set aside.

COOK'S TIP

Mussels can be prepared ahead of time and marinated for up to 24 hours. To serve, arrange the mussel shells on a bed of crushed ice, well-washed seaweed or even coarse salt to stop them from wobbling on the plate.

4 Discard any mussels with closed shells. With a small sharp knife, carefully remove the remaining mussels from their shells, reserving the half shells for serving. Add the mussels to the marinade. Toss the mussels to coat well, then cover and chill in the refrigerator for 6–8 hours or overnight, stirring gently every so often.

5 With a teaspoon, place one mussel with a little marinade in each shell. Arrange on a platter and cover until ready to serve.

Sautéed Mussels with Garlic and Herbs

These mussels are served without their shells, in a delicious paprika-flavored sauce. Eat them with toothpicks.

INGREDIENTS

Serves 4

2 pounds fresh mussels

1 lemon slice

6 tablespoons olive oil

2 shallots, finely chopped

1 garlic clove, finely chopped

1 tablespoon chopped fresh parsley

½ teaspoon sweet paprika

¼ teaspoon dried chile flakes

1 Scrub the mussels, discarding any damaged ones that do not close when tapped with a knife. Put the mussels in a large pan, with 1 cup water and the slice of lemon. Bring to a boil and cook for 3–4 minutes, removing the mussels as they open. Discard any that remain closed. Take the mussels out of the shells and drain on paper towels.

2 Heat the oil in a sauté pan, add the mussels and cook, stirring, for 1 minute. Remove from the pan. Add the shallots and garlic and cook, covered, over low heat for about 5 minutes or until soft. Remove from the heat and stir in the parsley, paprika and chile.

3 Return to the heat and stir in the mussels. Cook briefly. Remove from the heat and cover for a minute or two, to let the flavors mingle, before serving.

Shrimp Toasts

These crunchy sesame-topped toasts are simple to prepare using a food processor for the shrimp paste.

INGREDIENTS

Makes 64

8 ounces cooked, peeled shrimp, well
   drained and patted dry
1 egg white
2 scallions, chopped
1 teaspoon chopped fresh ginger
1 garlic clove, chopped
1 teaspoon cornstarch
½ teaspoon salt
½ teaspoon sugar
2–3 dashes hot pepper sauce
8 slices firm-textured white bread
4–5 tablespoons sesame seeds
vegetable oil, for frying
scallion pompom, to garnish

1 Put the first 9 ingredients in the bowl of a food processor and process until the mixture forms a smooth paste, occasionally scraping down the side of the bowl.

COOK'S TIP

You can prepare these in advance and heat them through in a hot oven before serving. Make sure they are really crisp and hot though, because they won't be nearly as enjoyable if there's no crunch when you bite them!

2 Spread the shrimp paste evenly on the bread slices, then sprinkle on the sesame seeds, pressing to make them stick. Remove the crusts, then cut each slice diagonally into 4 triangles, and each in half again. Make 64 triangles in total.

3 Heat 2 inches vegetable oil in a heavy saucepan or wok, until it is hot but not smoking. Fry the triangles in batches for 30–60 seconds, turning the toasts once. Drain on paper towels and keep hot in the oven while you cook the rest. Serve hot with the garnish.

Tuna in Rolled Red Bell Peppers

This savory combination originated in southern Italy. Roasted peppers have a sweet, smoky taste that combines particularly well with a robust fish like tuna. You could try canned mackerel instead.

INGREDIENTS

Serves 8–10

3 large red bell peppers

7-ounce can tuna fish, drained

2 tablespoons lemon juice

3 tablespoons olive oil

6 green or black olives, pitted and chopped

2 tablespoons chopped fresh parsley

1 garlic clove, finely chopped

1 celery stalk, very finely chopped

salt and ground black pepper

1 Place the peppers under a hot broiler, and turn occasionally until they are black and blistered on all sides. Remove from the heat and place in a plastic bag.

2 Let stand for 5 minutes, then peel. Cut the peppers into quarters, and remove the stems, seeds and pith.

3 Meanwhile, flake the tuna and combine with the lemon juice and oil. Stir in the olives, parsley, garlic and celery. Season with salt and plenty of ground black pepper.

4 Lay the pepper segments out flat, skin side down. Divide the tuna mixture equally among them. Spread it out, pressing it into an even layer. Roll up the peppers. Place the pepper rolls in the refrigerator for at least 1 hour. Just before serving, cut each roll in half with a sharp knife.

Smoked Trout Mousse in Cucumber Cups

This delicious creamy mousse can be made in advance and chilled for 2–3 days in the refrigerator. Serve it in crunchy cucumber cups, or simply with crudités, if you prefer.

INGREDIENTS

Makes about 24

¹/₂ cup cream cheese, softened

2 scallions, chopped

1–2 tablespoons, chopped fresh dill
or parsley

1 teaspoon horseradish sauce

8 ounces smoked trout fillets, flaked and
any fine bones removed

2–4 tablespoons heavy cream

salt, to taste

cayenne pepper, to taste

2 cucumbers

dill sprigs, to garnish

1 Put the cream cheese, scallions, dill or parsley, and horseradish sauce into a blender or the bowl of a food processor and process until well blended. Add the trout and process until smooth, scraping down the sides of the bowl once. With the machine running, pour in the cream through the feeder tube until a soft mousse-like mixture forms. Season, turn into a bowl and chill for 15 minutes.

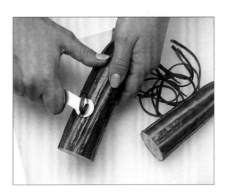

2 Using a zester or vegetable peeler, score the length of each cucumber to create a striped effect. Cut each cucumber into ³/₄-inch thick rounds. Using a small spoon or melon baller, scoop out the seeds from the center of each round.

3 Spoon the smoked trout mousse into a piping bag fitted with a medium star nozzle, and pipe swirls of the mixture into the prepared cucumber rounds. Chill until ready to serve. Garnish the cucumber cups with small sprigs of dill.

Foie Gras Pâté in Phyllo Cups

This is an extravagantly rich hors d'oeuvre—so save it for a special anniversary or celebration.

INGREDIENTS

Makes 24

3–6 sheets fresh or defrosted phyllo pastry

3 tablespoons butter, melted

8 ounces foie gras pâté or other fine liver pâté, at room temperature

4 tablespoons butter, softened

2–3 tablespoons Cognac or brandy (optional)

chopped pistachios, to garnish

2 Keeping the rest of the phyllo squares covered, place one square on a work surface and brush lightly with melted butter, then turn and brush the other side.

5 Bake the phyllo cups for 4–6 minutes, until crisp and golden, then remove and cool in the tin for 5 minutes. Carefully transfer each phyllo cup to a wire rack and let cool completely.

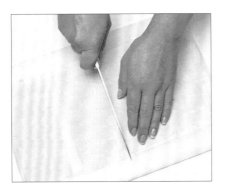

1 Preheat the oven to 400°F. Grease a muffin tin with 1½-inch cups. Stack the phyllo sheets on a work surface and cut into 2½-inch squares. Cover with a damp dish towel.

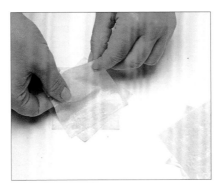

3 Butter a second square and place it over the first at an angle. Butter a third square and place at an angle over the first two sheets to form an uneven edge.

4 Press the layers into a cup of the muffin pan. Continue with the remaining pastry and butter until all the cups in the muffin tin have been filled.

6 In a small bowl, beat the pâté with the softened butter until smooth and well blended. Add the Cognac or brandy to taste, if using. Spoon into a piping bag fitted with a medium star nozzle and pipe a swirl into each cup. Sprinkle with pistachios. Chill until you are ready to serve.

COOK'S TIP

The pâté and pastry are best eaten soon after preparation. If preparing ahead of time and then chilling in the refrigerator, be sure to bring back to room temperature before serving.

Monti Cristo Triangles

*These opulent little sandwiches are
stuffed with ham, cheese and turkey,
dipped in egg, then fried in butter
and oil. They are rich, very filling—
and very popular too.*

INGREDIENTS

Makes 64

16 slices firm-textured thin-sliced
   white bread
½ cup butter, softened
8 slices oak-smoked ham
3–4 tablespoons whole-grain mustard
8 slices Gruyère or Emmenthal cheese
3–4 tablespoons mayonnaise
8 slices turkey or chicken breast
4–5 eggs
¼ cup milk
1 teaspoon Dijon mustard
vegetable oil, for frying
butter, for frying
salt and ground white pepper
pimiento-stuffed green olives, to garnish
parsley leaves, to garnish

1 Arrange 8 of the bread slices
on a work surface and spread
with half the softened butter. Lay a
slice of ham on each slice of bread
and spread with a little mustard.
Cover with a slice of Gruyère or
Emmenthal cheese and spread
with a little of the mayonnaise,
then cover with a slice of turkey or
chicken breast. Butter the rest of
the bread slices and use to top the
sandwiches. Cut off the crusts,
trimming to an even square.

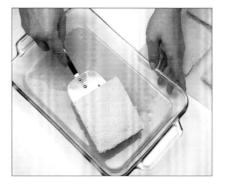

2 In a large shallow baking dish,
beat the eggs, milk and Dijon
mustard until well combined.
Season with salt and pepper. Soak
the sandwiches in the egg mixture
on both sides until the egg has
been absorbed.

3 Heat about ½ inch of oil with
a little butter in a large heavy
frying pan, until hot but not
smoking. Gently fry the sandwiches
in batches for 4–5 minutes, until
crisp and golden, turning once.
Add more oil and butter as
necessary. Drain on paper towels.

4 Transfer the sandwiches to a
cutting board and cut each
into 4 triangles, then each in half
again. Make 64 triangles in total.
Thread an olive and parsley leaf
onto a toothpick, then stick into
each triangle and serve
immediately while warm.

Potato Blinis

These light blinis originate from Russia, where they are served with caviar. Here they are topped with cream and smoked salmon.

INGREDIENTS

Serves 6

4 ounces maincrop potatoes, boiled and mashed

1 tablespoon easy-blend dried yeast

1½ cups all-purpose flour

oil, for greasing

6 tablespoons sour cream

6 slices smoked salmon

salt and ground black pepper

lemon slices, to garnish

COOK'S TIP

These small blinis can easily be prepared in advance and stored in the refrigerator until ready for use. Simply warm them through in a low oven.

1 In a large bowl, combine the potatoes, dried yeast, flour and 1¼ cups lukewarm water.

2 Let rise in a warm place for about 30 minutes, until the mixture has doubled in size.

3 Heat a nonstick frying pan and add a little oil. Drop spoonfuls of the mixture onto the preheated pan. Cook the blinis for 2 minutes, until lightly golden on the underside, toss with a spatula and cook on the second side for about 1 minute.

4 Season the blinis with some salt and pepper. Serve with a little sour cream and a small slice of smoked salmon folded on top. Garnish with a final grind of black pepper and a small slice of lemon.

Broiled Asparagus with Salt-cured Ham

Serve this tapas when asparagus is plentiful and not too expensive.

INGREDIENTS

Serves 4

6 slices of Serrano ham

12 asparagus spears

1 tablespoon olive oil

sea salt and coarsely ground black pepper

COOK'S TIP

If you can't find Serrano ham, use Italian prosciutto or Portuguese presunto.

1 Preheat the broiler to high. Halve each slice of ham lengthwise and wrap one half around each of the asparagus spears.

2 Brush the ham and asparagus lightly with oil and sprinkle with salt and pepper. Place on a broiler pan. Broil for 5–6 minutes, turning frequently, until the asparagus is tender but still firm. Serve immediately.

Dates Stuffed with Chorizo

This is a delicious combination from Spain, using fresh dates and spicy chorizo sausage.

Serves 4–6

2 ounces chorizo sausage

12 fresh dates, pitted

6 strips bacon

oil, for frying

all-purpose flour, for dusting

1 egg, beaten

1 cup fresh bread crumbs

1 Trim the ends of the chorizo sausage and then peel off the skin. Cut into three ¾-inch slices. Cut these in half lengthwise, then into quarters, giving 12 pieces.

2 Stuff each date with a piece of chorizo, closing the date around it. Stretch the bacon, by running the back of a knife along each strip. Cut each strip in half, widthwise. Wrap a piece of bacon around each date and secure with a wooden toothpick.

3 In a deep pan, heat ½ inch of oil. Dust the dates with flour, dip them in the beaten egg, then coat in bread crumbs. Fry the dates in the hot oil, turning them, until golden. Remove the dates with a draining spoon, and drain on paper towels. Serve immediately.

Crispy Spring Rolls

These small and dainty spring rolls are ideal served as appetizers or as cocktail snacks. If desired, you could replace the mushrooms with chicken or pork and the carrots with shrimp.

INGREDIENTS

Makes 40 rolls

8 ounces fresh beansprouts

4 ounces small leeks or scallions

4 ounces carrots

4 ounces bamboo shoots, sliced

4 ounces mushrooms

3–4 tablespoons vegetable oil

1 teaspoon salt

1 teaspoon light brown sugar

1 tablespoon light soy sauce

1 tablespoon Chinese rice wine or
   dry sherry

20 frozen spring roll skins, defrosted

1 tablespoon cornstarch paste (see
   Cook's Tip)

all-purpose flour, for dusting

oil, for deep-frying

1 Cut all the vegetables into thin shreds, roughly the same size and shape as the beansprouts.

2 Heat the oil in a wok and stir-fry the vegetables for about 1 minute. Add the salt, sugar, soy sauce and wine or sherry and continue stirring the vegetables for 1½–2 minutes. Remove and drain away the excess liquid, then let cool.

3 To make the spring rolls, cut each spring roll skin in half diagonally, then place about a tablespoonful of the vegetable mixture one-third of the way down on the skin, with the triangle pointing away from you.

> ### COOK'S TIP
>
> To make cornstarch paste, mix 4 parts cornstarch with about 5 parts cold water until smooth.

4 Lift the lower edge over the filling and roll once.

5 Fold in both ends and roll again, then brush the upper pointed edge with a little cornstarch paste, and roll into a neat package. Lightly dust a tray with flour and place the spring rolls on the tray with the flapside underneath.

6 To cook, heat the oil in a wok or deep-fryer until hot, then reduce the heat to low. Deep-fry the spring rolls in batches (about 8–10 at a time) for 2–3 minutes or until golden and crispy, then remove and drain. Serve the spring rolls hot with a dipping sauce, such as soy sauce, or mixed salt and pepper.

Chorizo Pastry Puffs

These flaky pastry puffs, filled with spicy chorizo sausage and grated cheese, make a really superb accompaniment to a glass of cold sherry or beer. You can use any type of hard cheese for the puffs, but for best results, choose a mild variety, as the chorizo has plenty of flavor.

INGREDIENTS

Serves 8

8 ounces puff pastry, thawed if frozen

4 ounces cured chorizo sausage,
   finely chopped

$\frac{1}{2}$ cup grated cheese

1 small egg, beaten

1 teaspoon paprika

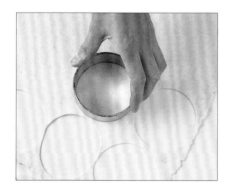

1 Roll out the pastry thinly on a floured work surface. Using a 3-inch cutter, stamp out as many rounds as possible, then re-roll the trimmings, if necessary, and stamp out more rounds to make 16 in all.

2 Preheat the oven to 450°F. Put the chopped chorizo sausage and grated cheese in a bowl and toss together lightly.

3 Lay one of the pastry rounds in the palm of your hand and place a little of the chorizo mixture on the center.

4 Using your other hand, pinch the edges of the pastry together along the top to seal, as when making a miniature patty. Repeat the process with the remaining rounds to make a total of 16 puffs in all.

5 Place the pastries on a nonstick baking sheet and brush lightly with the beaten egg. Using a small sifter or tea strainer, dust the tops lightly with a little of the paprika.

6 Bake the pastries for 10–12 minutes, until puffed and golden brown. Transfer the pastries to a wire rack. Let cool for 5 minutes, then serve the chorizo pastry puffs warm, dusted with the remaining paprika.

Samosas

These tasty snacks are enjoyed the world over. Throughout the East, they are sold by street vendors, and eaten at any time of day. Phyllo pastry can be used if a lighter, flakier texture is preferred.

INGREDIENTS

Makes about 20

1 package 10-inch square spring roll
    wrappers, thawed if frozen
2 tablespoons all-purpose flour, mixed
    into a paste with water
vegetable oil, for deep frying
cilantro leaves, to garnish

For the filling

2 tablesponns ghee or unsalted butter
1 small onion finely chopped
$\frac{1}{2}$-inch piece fresh ginger root, peeled and
    chopped
1 garlic glove, crushed
$\frac{1}{2}$ teaspoon chili powder
1 large potato, about 8 ounces, cooked
    until just tender and finely diced
$\frac{1}{2}$ cup cauliflower florets, lightly cooked,
    chopped into small pieces
$\frac{1}{2}$ cup frozen peas, thawed
1–2 teaspoons garam masala
1 tablespoon chopped cilantro (leaves
    and stems)
squeeze of lemon juice
salt

1 Heat the ghee or butter in a large frying pan and fry the onion, ginger and garlic for 5 minutes, until the onion has softened but not browned. Add the chili powder and cook for 1 minute, then stir in the potato, cauliflower and peas. Sprinkle with garam masala and set aside to cool. Stir in the chopped cilantro, lemon juice and salt.

2 Cut the spring roll wrappers into three strips (or two for larger samosas). Brush the edges with a little of the flour paste. Place a small spoonful of filling about ¾-inch in from the edge of one strip. Fold one corner over the filling to make a triangle and continue this folding until the entire strip has been used and a triangular pastry has been formed. Seal any open edges with more flour and water paste, if necessary, adding more water if the paste is very thick.

3 Heat the oil for deep-frying to 375°F and fry the samosas, a few at a time, until golden and crisp. Drain well on paper towels and serve hot garnished with cilantro leaves.

COOK'S TIP

Prepare samosas in advance by frying until just cooked through and draining. Cook in hot oil for a few minutes to brown and drain again before serving.

Rice Triangles

These rice shapes—Onigari—are very popular in Japan. You can put anything you want in the rice, so you could invent your own Onigiri.

Serves 4

1 salmon steak

1 tablespoon salt

4 cups freshly cooked sushi rice

¼ cucumber, seeded and cut
   into matchsticks

½ sheet yaki-nori seaweed, cut into four
   equal strips

white and black sesame seeds, for
   sprinkling

1 Broil the salmon steaks on each side, until the flesh flakes easily when tested with the tip of a sharp knife. Set aside to cool while you make other onigiri. When the salmon is cold, flake it, discarding any skin and bones.

2 Put the salt in a bowl. Spoon an eighth of the warm cooked rice into a small rice bowl. Make a hole in the middle of the rice and put in a few cucumber matchsticks. Smooth the rice to cover.

3 Wet the palms of both hands with cold water, then rub the salt evenly on your palms.

4 Empty the rice and cucumbers from the bowl onto one hand. Use both hands to shape the rice into a triangular shape, using firm but not heavy pressure, and making sure that the cucumber is encased by the rice. Make three more rice triangles the same way.

5 Mix the flaked salmon into the remaining rice, then shape it into triangles as before.

6 Wrap a strip of yakinori around each of the cucumber triangles. Sprinkle sesame seeds on the salmon triangles.

COOK'S TIP

Always use warm rice to make the triangles. Let them cool completely and wrap each in aluminum foil or plastic wrap.

Mini Sausage Rolls

These miniature versions of old-fashioned sausage rolls are always popular—the Parmesan cheese gives them an extra special flavor.

INGREDIENTS

Makes about 48

1 tablespoon butter

1 onion, finely chopped

12 ounces good quality sausage meat

1 tablespoon dried mixed herbs such as oregano, thyme, sage, tarragon or dill

1 ounce finely chopped pistachios (optional)

12 ounces puff pastry, thawed if frozen

4–6 tablespoons freshly grated Parmesan cheese

salt and ground black pepper

1 egg, lightly beaten, for glazing

poppy seeds, sesame seeds, fennel seeds and aniseeds, for sprinkling

1 In a small frying pan, over medium heat, melt the butter. Add the onion and cook for about 5 minutes, until softened. Remove from the heat and cool. Put the onion, sausage meat, herbs, salt and pepper and nuts (if using) in a mixing bowl and stir together until completely blended.

2 Divide the sausage mixture into 4 equal portions and roll into thin sausages measuring about 10 inches long. Set aside.

3 On a lightly floured surface, roll out the pastry to about ⅛ inch thick. Cut the pastry into 4 strips 10 x 3 inches long. Place a long sausage on each pastry strip and sprinkle each with a little Parmesan cheese.

COOK'S TIP

Phyllo pastry can be used instead of puff pastry for a very light effect. Depending on the size of the phyllo sheets, cut into 8 pieces 10 x 3 inches. Brush 4 of the sheets with a little melted butter or vegetable oil and place a second pastry sheet on top. Place one sausage log on each of the four layered sheets and roll up and bake as above.

4 Brush one long edge of each of the pastry strips with the egg glaze and roll up to enclose each sausage. Set them seam-side down and press gently to seal. Brush each with the egg glaze and sprinkle with one type of seeds. Repeat with remaining pastry strips, using different seeds.

5 Preheat the oven to 425°F. Lightly grease a large baking sheet. Cut each of the pastry logs into 1-inch lengths and arrange on the baking sheet. Bake for about 15 minutes, until the pastry is crisp and brown. Serve warm or let cool before serving.

Sushi-style Tuna Cubes

These tasty tuna cubes are easier to prepare than classic Japanese sushi but retain the same fresh taste.

Makes about 24

1½ pounds fresh tuna steak, about
¾-inch thick
1 large red bell pepper, seeded and cut
into ¾-inch pieces
sesame seeds, for sprinkling

For the marinade

1–2 tablespoons lemon juice
½ teaspoon salt
½ teaspoon sugar
½ teaspoon wasabi paste
½ cup olive or vegetable oil
2 tablespoons chopped fresh cilantro

For the soy dipping sauce

7 tablespoons soy sauce
1 tablespoon rice wine vinegar
1 teaspoon lemon juice
1–2 scallions, finely chopped
1 teaspoon sugar
2–3 dashes Asian hot chili oil or hot
pepper sauce

2 Prepare the marinade. In a small bowl, stir the lemon juice with the salt, sugar and wasabi paste. Slowly whisk in the oil until well blended and slightly creamy. Stir in the cilantro. Pour onto the tuna cubes and toss to coat. Cover and marinate for about 40 minutes in a cool place.

3 Meanwhile, prepare the soy dipping sauce. Combine all the ingredients in a small bowl and stir until well blended. Cover until ready to serve.

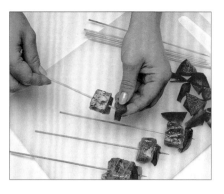

4 Preheat the broiler and line a baking sheet with aluminum foil. Thread a cube of tuna then a piece of pepper onto each skewer and arrange on the baking sheet.

5 Sprinkle with sesame seeds and broil for 3–5 minutes, turning once or twice, until just beginning to color but still pink inside. Serve with the soy dipping sauce.

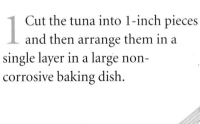

1 Cut the tuna into 1-inch pieces and then arrange them in a single layer in a large non-corrosive baking dish.

COOK'S TIP

Wasabi is a hot, pungent Japanese horseradish available in powder form (that has to be reconstituted) and as paste in a tube at gourmet and Japanese food stores.

Lamb Tikka

Creamy yogurt and ground nuts go wonderfully with the spices in these little Indian meatballs.

INGREDIENTS

Makes about 20

1 pound lamb fillet

2 scallions, chopped

For the marinade

1½ cups plain yogurt

1 tablespoon ground almonds,
    cashews or peanuts

1 tablespoon vegetable oil

2–3 garlic cloves, finely chopped

juice of 1 lemon

1 teaspoon garam masala or curry powder

½ teaspoon ground cardamom

¼ teaspoon cayenne pepper

1–2 tablespoons chopped fresh mint

1 To prepare the marinade, stir together the marinade ingredients. In a separate small bowl, reserve about ½ cup of the mixture to use as a dipping sauce for the meatballs.

2 Cut the lamb into small pieces and put in the bowl of a food processor with the scallions. Process, using the pulse action, until the meat is finely chopped. Add 2–3 tablespoons of the marinade and process again.

3 Test to see if the mixture holds together by pinching a little between your fingertips. Add a little more marinade if necessary, but do not make the mixture too wet and soft.

4 With moistened palms, form the meat mixture into slightly oval-shaped balls, measuring about 1½-inch long, and arrange in a shallow baking dish. Spoon on the remaining marinade and chill the meatballs in the refrigerator for 8–10 hours or overnight.

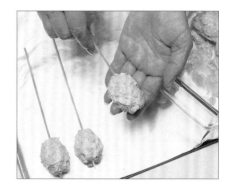

5 Preheat the broiler and line a baking sheet with aluminum foil. Thread each meatball onto a skewer and arrange on the baking sheet. Broil for 4–5 minutes, turning them occasionally, until crisp and golden on all sides. Serve with the reserved marinade as a dipping sauce.

Index